Big Data

T0335546

The internet has launched the world into an era into which enormous amounts of data are generated every day through technologies with both positive and negative consequences. This often refers to *big data*. This book explores big data in organisations operating in the criminology and criminal justice fields.

Big data entails a major disruption in the ways we think about and do things, which certainly applies to most organisations including those operating in the criminology and criminal justice fields. Big data is currently disrupting processes in most organisations – how different organisations collaborate with one another, how organisations develop products or services, how organisations can identify, recruit, and evaluate talent, how organisations can make better decisions based on empirical evidence rather than intuition, and how organisations can quickly implement any transformation plan, to name a few.

All these processes are important to tap into, but two underlying processes are critical to establish a foundation that will permit organisations to flourish and thrive in the era of big data – creating a culture more receptive to big data and implementing a systematic data analytics-driven process within the organisation.

Written in a clear and direct style, this book will appeal to students and scholars in criminology, criminal justice, sociology, and cultural studies but also to government agencies, corporate and non-corporate organisations, or virtually any other institution impacted by big data.

Benoit Leclerc is an Associate Professor of Criminology and Criminal Justice at Griffith University, Brisbane, Australia. His research interests include the development and application of procedural analysis (i.e., crime scripting) for purposes of crime investigation, detection, and prevention. He is leading several research projects with corrections and police organisations. With Clifford Shearing and Ross Homel, he is the cofounding editor of *Criminology at the Edge*, an annual edited volume series in criminology (Routledge). Recent publications appeared in *Criminal Justice and Behavior*, *Crime & Delinquency*, the *Journal of Research in Crime*, and *Delinquency and Sexual Abuse*.

Jesse Cale is an Associate Professor of Criminology in the School of Criminology and Criminal Justice at Griffith University and an Adjunct Associate Professor in the School of Social Sciences at the University of New South Wales in Australia. His main areas of research involve the causes and consequences of sexual violence, developmental criminology, and criminal justice policy and evaluation. He is a chief investigator on several large-scale research grants in Australia funded by the Australian Research Council and different state governments and agencies examining the development of delinquency and criminal offending and the effectiveness of criminal justice policy responses to crime.

Criminology at the Edge
Benoit Leclerc
Ross Homel
Clifford Shearing
Griffith University, Australia

Over the last few decades, criminology has become known for its rigorous research methods and innovative analyses as well as for the development and testing of traditional and new theories. Criminology, as a science, has become known for its empirical-based theorizing and its dedication to enable this knowledge to contribute effectively to realizing the goal of creating safe and just societies. This interdisciplinary series explores innovative developments and imagined futures within criminology.

The objective of this series is to expand the boundaries of criminology and facilitate, encourage and disseminate the fruits of a thorough and meticulous discussions of the most important emerging trends within criminology. Innovative criminologists will be encouraged to take risks as they imagine a criminology for the 21st Century, and to think outside existing criminological boxes.

The Future of Rational Choice for Crime Prevention
Edited by Danielle M. Reynald and Benoit Leclerc

Criminology and the Anthropocene
Edited by Cameron Holley and Clifford Shearing

Big Data
Edited by Benoit Leclerc and Jesse Cale

For more information about this series, please visit: www.routledge.com/ Criminology-at-the-Edge/book-series/CATE

Big Data

Edited by Benoit Leclerc and Jesse Cale

Routledge
Taylor & Francis Group

LONDON AND NEW YORK

First published 2020
by Routledge
2 Park Square, Milton Park, Abingdon, Oxon OX14 4RN

and by Routledge
52 Vanderbilt Avenue, New York, NY 10017

Routledge is an imprint of the Taylor & Francis Group, an informa business

© 2020 selection and editorial matter, Benoit Leclerc and Jesse Cale; individual chapters, the contributors

British Library Cataloguing-in-Publication Data
A catalogue record for this book is available from the British Library

Library of Congress Cataloging-in-Publication Data
Names: LeClerc, Benoit, editor.
Title: Big data / Benoit Leclerc and Jesse Cale.
Description: Milton Park, Abingdon, Oxon ; New York, NY : Routledge, 2020. | Series: Criminology at the edge | Includes bibliographical references and index.
Identifiers: LCCN 2019048736 | ISBN 9781138492783 (hbk) | ISBN 9781351029704 (ebk)
Subjects: LCSH: Criminology—Data processing. | Big data.
Classification: LCC HV6025 .B527 2020 | DDC 364.0285/57—dc23
LC record available at https://lccn.loc.gov/2019048736

ISBN: 978-1-138-49278-3 (hbk)
ISBN: 978-1-351-02970-4 (ebk)

Typeset in Times New Roman
by Apex CoVantage, LLC

Such a creative journey would not have been possible without the loves of my life, Alba, Laetitia, and Maia.

– Benoit

For my two loves, Stacy and Parker.

– Jesse

Contents

Contributors

Martin A. Andresen is a Professor in the School of Criminology and Director of the Institute for Canadian Urban Research Studies at Simon Fraser University. Prof. Andresen's research interests are in crime and places, environmental criminology, the geography of crime, spatial crime analysis, and applied spatial statistics and geographical information analysis. He is an Associate Editor for Journal of Quantitative Criminology, and an Editorial Board member for the following journals: Journal of Criminal Justice; Journal of Quantitative Criminology; International Criminal Justice Review; Criminology, Criminal Justice, Law & Society; and Methodological Innovations.

Matt DeLisi is College of Liberal Arts and Sciences Dean's Professor, Coordinator of Criminal Justice Studies, Professor in the Department of Sociology, and Faculty Affiliate with the Center for the Study of Violence at Iowa State University. Dr. DeLisi is also Visiting Professor at the University of Huddersfield in the United Kingdom. A Fellow of the Academy of Criminal Justice Sciences, Professor DeLisi is among the most prolific and highly-cited criminologists in the world.

Charlotte Gerritsen is a computational criminologist. She currently holds an assistant professor position in Social AI at the Faculty of Sciences of the VU University Amsterdam. With a master's degree in Criminology and a PhD in Artificial Intelligence she focuses her research on applying techniques from the field of AI to study criminological phenomena. These techniques include among others agent-based simulation, serious gaming and sentiment analysis. She currently works on a large personal grant project focusing on real time prediction of aggressive crowd behavior based on social media feeds.

Uwe Glässer is a professor of Computing Science, Simon Fraser University, BC, Canada. His research interests range from formal engineering methods for mathematical modeling of discrete dynamic systems to interdisciplinary applications of computer science in situation analysis and anomaly detection, big data intelligence, criminal network analysis, maritime security and cybersecurity of critical infrastructure. Virtually all of this work builds on interdisciplinary research collaborations with national and international partners in the public and the private sector, including academic institutions, high-tech industry, Defence R&D, law enforcement, intelligence agencies, and municipalities.

Alexandra Green received her BAH in political studies from Queen's University in Canada and is currently pursuing a Master's degree in Infrastructure Protection and International Security at Carleton University. During her time at Queen's University she was awarded an undergraduate fellowship, the John Rae award, the Women in Defence and Security Scholarship, the Chancellor's Scholarship, and was placed on the Dean's List with Distinction. She has been engaged in research projects examining border security, terrorist resourcing, countering violent extremism, policing, and critical infrastructure. She has been published in the Journal of Money Laundering Control.

Melissa Green (PhD) is Professor of Psychiatry at the University of New South Wales, Sydney, and an affiliated scientist at Neuroscience Research Australia (NeuRA). Her research spans multiple disciplines including molecular genetics, neuroscience, social science, and epidemiology, with a focus on determining modifiable social and biological risk factors for the development of mental illness and other adverse outcomes across the life-course.

Thomas J. Holt is a Professor in the School of Criminal Justice at Michigan State University whose research focuses on computer hacking, malware, and the role of the Internet in facilitating all manner of crime and deviance.

Jin R. Lee is a PhD student at the School of Criminal Justice at Michigan State University. His research interests are in cybercrime, online interpersonal violence, cybersecurity, crime and media, and race and gender inequality within the criminal justice system.

Christian Leuprecht is Class of 1965 Professor in Leadership, Department of Political Science and Economics, Royal Military College of Canada. Cross-appointed, Department of Political Studies and the School of Policy Studies, Queen's University, where he is affiliated with both, the Queen's Centre for International and Defence Policy and the Institute of Intergovernmental Relations, he is also Adjunct Research Professor, Australian Graduate School of Policing and Security, at Charles Sturt University. He has held visiting positions in North America (Bicentennial Chair in Canadian Studies, Yale University), Europe (Eisenhower Fellow, NATO Defence College), and Australia (Matthew Flinders Fellow, Flinders University). He holds appointments to the board of the German Institute for Defence and Strategic Studies and the Police Services Board of the City of Kingston.

David Skillicorn is a Professor in the School of Computing at Queen's University. His undergraduate degree is from the University of Sydney and his Ph.D. from the University of Manitoba. He is also an Adjunct Professor at the Royal Military College of Canada. He has published extensively in the area of adversarial data analytics and has also been involved in interdisciplinary research on radicalization, terrorism, and fraud.

Mohammad A. Tayebi is a Post-doctoral researcher at the School of Computing Science, Simon Fraser University, BC, Canada. His general research interests are in the areas of machine learning, data mining and social network analysis with focus on social computing, cyber security and computational criminology fields.

Foreword

Understanding big data is a long journey – a journey that is leading many organisations to scratch their heads about the best ways to understand what it means for them and what impact it will have on their systems, processes, and people, regardless of the industry and business function within the organisation. Hopefully, many organisations can also see the potential of using big data to improve what they do and how they do it. The bad news is that there are important challenges to overcome for most organisations. The good news is that we can overcome these challenges. This volume is innovative and future-looking in its approach and was designed with the hope of generating solutions to overcome important challenges generated by big data in criminology and criminal justice-related organisations and beyond.

Three important features best describe this volume. First, even if this volume sits in the discipline of criminology and criminal justice, we looked at what is known on big data, its challenges, and potential solutions through the lens of the business literature. Mostly sourced from the *Harvard Business Review* and *McKinsey Quarterly*, the literature not only led us to a much deeper understanding of the challenges associated with big data but also provided important insights to make big data work for organisations across any industry. We realised that the business literature is arguably much more robust when it comes to understanding the potential challenges and benefits posed by big data compared to the social sciences, and more specifically, criminology and criminal justice – despite the high quality of data analytics utilised in much of criminology. Second, in a very inductive manner, we invited contributors to participate in this volume with the hope that important themes around big data would emerge organically across the volume and assist us to some extent in making sense of which steps organisations could take next for improving their practices. Third, it became obvious through reading the contributions of this volume that key challenges related to culture and data analytics processes are critical not only in the world outside of criminology and criminal justice but also in this field quite specifically. Drawing on what is known in the business literature, we then developed step-by-step generic roadmaps for organisations to 1) create a culture more receptive to data and 2) implement a systematic data analytics-driven process. The roadmaps are applied to criminology and criminal justice-related organisations but are flexible in nature, and thus can be adapted if need be to any organisation including government agencies, corporate and non-corporate organisations, universities, research institutions, and virtually any other type of organisation.

Rare is the opportunity to create a contribution that uncovers common challenges that cut across organisations or even industries and develop generic roadmaps to overcome these challenges in a systematic way that any organisation can readily understand. Without touching on everything that has to be said on big data (this would require many other volumes), this volume covers the essential foundation and starting point to actually engage and work with any organisation to overcome critical challenges related to big data and generate better outcomes for them.

Benoit Leclerc and Jesse Cale
Associate Professors, Griffith Criminology Institute, Griffith University,
Brisbane, Australia

1 Big data in criminology and criminal justice through the lens of the business literature

Jesse Cale, Benoit Leclerc, and Francis Gil

Introduction

Whether in government agencies, corporate and non-corporate organisations, large firms, academia, politics, and so on, the internet has launched the world into an era into which enormous amounts of data are generated every day through technologies with both positive and negative consequences. This often refers to *big data*. But what is big data, how is it relevant in general, and, more specifically, for criminology and criminal justice? Speculations on the implications of big data for the field have begun, but there is no solid consensus in the criminological literature about what exactly big data refers to, and how it will impact theory, research, and most importantly, practice. Big data typically implies an abundance of data and new processes, such as data mining and data analytics, which provides virtually anyone using data with the opportunity to generate new discoveries or upscale an organisation's capabilities. Most importantly, big data brings challenges to organisations and innovative embedded systematic solutions are much needed to overcome these challenges so that organisations can thrive and prosper in a safe environment.

This chapter is divided into two major sections. In the first section we primarily revisit how big data is defined while trying to make sense of the concept for clarification and 'industry' consensus purposes. We then discuss two critical challenges that cut across organisations and industries. One fundamental challenge is culture. In any organisation, culture is a dimension that has been examined in depth because of the benefits associated with 'getting it right' and the costs of 'getting it wrong'. Any organisation should typically be seeking to align its mission with its people and culture and vice versa. Therefore, if the culture of one organisation is not receptive to big data, making the best of data for that organisation will be twice as challenging. Another relevant challenge is related to the applications of big data and data analytics. Suffice it to say that having access to an enormous amount of data is meaningless for an organisation unless these data are of a certain quality, can be utilised effectively, and that the 'entry point' (i.e., formulating questions to address) and 'exit point' (i.e., interpretation and dissemination of findings) of the process of data analytics are completed with diligence.

After discussing the importance of culture and the process of big data and data analytics in the first section, the second section of this chapter consists of looking essentially at the challenges noted earlier but with a specific focus on the fields of criminology and criminal justice. Indeed, this discussion likely carries much relevance for other academic disciplines and industries as well. We examine big data and its challenges in the context of criminology and criminal justice while referring at different points to each of the six contributions included as part of this volume on big data.

Big data – what is it?

Big data is a concept that has been 'defined' in various ways and may be understood differently by people working in different industries or even within the same industry. More so, it is often understood differently within the same organisation especially by people who have had very little exposure to data. Big data generally concerns the abundance of data generated through technology and the internet of things – social media, mobile phone usage, any personal information held by banks, the government or any organisation in the public sector, and so on. In this sense, it also refers to an era dominated by easy access to information and disruptive technology. Big data may also refer to the movement taken by large organisations toward using data to become more productive and profitable. McAfee and Brynjolfsson (2012) specifically speak of a movement, which uses three key characteristics to define big data, that is, volume, velocity, and variety. *Volume* implies the massive amount of data generated every day while *velocity* refers to how fast the data can be created from various sources of information. *Variety* concerns the number of infinite potential sources of data ranging from simple messages posted on social media to GPS signals produced from mobile phones. In the end, how we define big data is significant to the extent that people across organisations and industries should be able to discuss the challenges and solutions on how to make the best of data. Importantly, defining big data may assist in educating people not generally exposed to data and make them aware of not only the risks and challenges associated with an approach favouring the use of data but also its benefits.

To us, it is important to approach big data as referring not only to the abundance of data in our societies but also to its immense potential for improving knowledge in a broad sense for the evolution, safety and well-being of societies – to help societies function better individually and in synergy in the context of a constantly evolving world. We offer a deliberately optimistic definition with the mindset that data should be used for the good of all. Of course, we do remain aware of the challenges and risks posed by 'too easy' access to sensitive data, for instance, or flawed analytics, in particular, that could lead to decisions with negative outcomes. Simply think of criminology and criminal justice. Child exploitation, fraud, money laundering, bullying, identity theft, human trafficking, and so on can have disastrous consequences that are facilitated by technology. Big data also provide new opportunities for people with ill intentions. How can we get the best of data while neutralising its worst potential then? This question is beyond the scope of this volume but helps us frame the volume in a more constructive manner for readers. It makes us remember and appreciate the numerous ramifications generated by big data. In our view, it is wiser to engage with data rather than resist it, especially given the nature and extent of problems and crimes that can emerge from it. In the next section we discuss two major challenges at the foundation of big data – two challenges that cut across organisations and industries and into which solutions for addressing crime problems should be embedded. These two challenges represent a fundamental starting point for any organisation regardless of their mission, objectives, and values.

Big data challenges

Shaping the culture

Culture is one of the most critical dimensions for success in any organisation. If the people within one organisation are not working as a group (or a team ideally), and in a similar 'headspace', that organisation will not progress as effectively as it could otherwise. Arguably, if the culture of one organisation is flexible and receptive to transformation then it should be relatively straightforward to take on novel directions. However, in any organisation, some people are commonly reluctant to changes as it puts them out of their comfort zone – they may simply be intimidated by the changes for fear of new role responsibilities, losing privileges, or even losing their job. A first and common challenge across organisations and industries in relation to big data and data analytics is also the culture of an organisation (e.g., Diaz, Rowshankish, & Saleh, 2018; McAfee & Brynjolfsson, 2012). McAfee and Brynjolfsson (2012) argue that many organisations need to stop pretending to be more data-driven than they actually are. Other organisations may be simply intimidated by technology to get into the data space or fear some negative consequences from adopting data-driven approaches, such as intrusions to privacy and risks related to sensitive information leakage. Some organisations may simply not understand the potential of an approach that encompasses the use of empirical data. Perhaps most importantly, people must be educated about the advantages, challenges, and risks related to using data so that they do not feel intimidated by it and understand its potential. This process brings the importance of shaping culture and bringing everyone together for a common purpose on how to make the best of data. From this point in time on, big data can only evolve and it is critical to accept this reality for making positive contributions to society but also better addressing challenges and problems that big data will continue to generate.

Diaz et al. (2018) point out that a data culture is what is in fact lacking in most organisations in the first place. Diaz and his colleagues present several principles that favour a healthy data culture in organisations. One principle refers to 'culture catalysts', that is, people who have the ability to bridge data capabilities and day-to-day knowledge to the operations of an organisation. The idea is that these people should lead the way as they can understand how an organisation could benefit from data. This principle taps into two important problems that lead organisations to failure when trying to incorporate data analytics into their operations (Fleming, Fountaine, Henke, & Saleh, 2018). The first problem emerges when an organisation lacks what they called 'analytics translators'. Essentially these are the people who represent 'culture catalysts' – those who have both business and data knowledge and can translate organisational needs to data analysts. There is an absolute need to have these people in the organisation and they should be recruited from within and outside the organisation (see the fourth principle in the next paragraph). The second problem taps into the importance of integrating analytics into the core of the organisation. If analytics works in isolation (i.e., not in synergy with other departments, divisions, or business functions) – the potential benefits of big data will decrease dramatically, and the risks of negatives consequences, such as errors in decision-making processes will be more likely.

A second related principle noted by Diaz et al. (2018) is data democratisation, which implies that people should get excited about the prospects of using data before embarking into the journey. This can be achieved through providing people with easy access and opportunities to interact with data and eventually, with time, people will start understanding and appreciating the benefits of it and believing in it – this speaks of practical and repeated exposure to data. The third principle raises awareness on the risk of data analytics of not generating positive outcomes for the organisation. The risk of getting analytics wrong always exists, which requires ongoing monitoring to check whether what has been generated actually makes sense for the organisation before decisions are made. A fourth principle involves marrying talent and culture. This principle refers to integrating the right talent (what is needed to embed a culture that favours the utilisation of data) through recruiting new people and upskilling people already employed by the organisation. Choosing the right people to lead data initiatives will be crucial to set up the foundation for a sustainable direction. In addition, analytics roles should be clearly defined within the organisation – people in the organisation should be aware of how the needs in analytics are covered and by whom (Fleming et al., 2018). A fifth principle – one that has been raised as critical by most authors in the data space – involves getting the ongoing support from the C-suites, board or other decision makers in the organisation. Conversations between the decision makers and the people leading data initiatives are essential to obtain a high level of commitment from decision makers, which in turn can generate a greater level of awareness to avoid negative consequences in the process. In the end, one ultimate objective of using empirical data is to enhance the capacity of decision makers to make more informed decisions for the organisation – making decisions driven by evidence rather than intuition (McAfee & Brynjolfsson, 2012). The principles outlined here are all relevant and interconnected. For instance, getting the right people – for example the 'culture catalysts' – will favour data democratisation, which obviously will be greatly facilitated if the decision makers clearly understand and support data initiatives. Furthermore, shaping the culture of the organisation requires these elements to work in synergy for success.

Groysberg, Lee, Price, and Yo-Jud Cheng (2018) outline a three-step process to adopt in order to set up culture targets for shaping cultures. The first step refers to understanding the current culture through its history and heritage as well as its strengths. This step is critical for an organisation because a solid historical foundation could be used for positive reinforcement and serves as evidence that its people are capable of embarking on new initiatives. The second step involves considering the strategy and the environment in which the strategy is being executed. This refers to shaping the culture according to the strategy chosen by the organisation to make the best of big data. For example, if the strategy is to build evidence-based knowledge on how an organisation is performing in attracting new and retaining current customers, the people should be aware of how the data will assist in understanding how the organisation is performing with customers and then, in turn, accept and support the strategy. The third step requires framing this transformation as an organisational priority to solve problems and create value within the organisation, not as a 'culture change' initiative as such. This step is highly valuable as 'transforming' the culture of one organisation could be perceived as a threat by some of its people because it will put them at the forefront of the new direction that the organisation is seeking to take. However, if the focus rather is put on the value that will be created by changing direction, that is, on positive and tangible outcomes, people may prove to be more receptive to it. As part of such a program, hiring new employees that fit with a culture and its mission in which big data is embraced is another strategy that organisations often adopt (Kell & Carrott, 2005) – a principle also discussed by Diaz et al. (2018). As pointed out by Bernik (2001), if one needs to fix an organisation and guide it toward a more successful path, the focus should arguably be put on the people first, which we believe is absolutely critical.

Providing that culture is receptive to big data and data analytics, data can provide an exceptional competitive advantage to organisations dedicated to it (Boudreau & Ramstad, 2003; Davenport, Harris, & Shapiro, 2010). As an illustration, applied to talent management within an organisation, Davenport et al. (2010) identify six relevant areas for the application of talent analytics, such as human-capital investments, analytical HR, and workforce forecasts. First and foremost, instead of relying on intuition, executives can use evidence-based knowledge from talent analytics to make important decisions about people in the organisation. Data are likely to lead to more optimal decisions and thus better outcomes for organisations (McAfee & Brynjolfsson, 2012). For instance, data analytics can assist in identifying the skills and interests of staff and link those to high performance. Then staff can be moved accordingly into roles that maximise their own success and as a result, generate better outcomes for the organisation (Davenport et al., 2010). Too often, organisations put skilled staff into the wrong role for convenience purposes or due to a lack of general competence into making critical decisions or understanding the mission of the organisation. Data on motivation and personal competencies could also help design strategies to improve workplace climate and, indirectly, staff performance. Such data can provide deep insights into the 'headspace' of staff and how well they are working as a 'team'. With data analytics skills, human resources management may also have a better chance to gain a seat at the executives table to actively participate in the organisation as a strategic/transformational partner (Lawler, Levenson, & Boudreau, 2004; McAfee & Brynjolfsson, 2012). However, once again, Davenport et al. (2010) indicate that executives themselves are often sceptical of examining human behaviour (probably because the execution of strategies in this regard is often poor in organisations), which brings us back to the importance of examining culture in the first place. In this context, leaders who support the use of human-capital insights must foster a culture to allow for experimentation and mistakes and promote the benefits of evidence-based knowledge over intuition (see also Court, 2015). In fact, Davenport et al. (2010) point out that the most important factor for success of talent analytics within an organisation is the commitment of the leaders to this approach. And to support commitment is to create or facilitate a culture of inquiry not advocacy (Davenport, 2013).

The process underlying big data and data analytics

Beyond having access to massive amounts of data, what may first come to mind when thinking data analytics is the knowledge of programming or conducting statistical analysis to uncover insights from data. This goal can be achieved within many organisations or outsourced in a relatively straightforward manner. However, when it comes to analytics, there is a more pressing need/challenge for organisations. Davenport's (2013) decision-making process map showcases the importance of this step (Figure 1.1). First and foremost, what is the organisation trying to address for its benefits? In other words, what is the question that the organisation is seeking to answer? Before anything else, the organisation must be aware of what issue or challenge they are trying to tap into, and this must be translated into a research question(s) that can be addressed by the data at hand. This research question must be an appropriate question – clear and specific enough for the data to uncover insights (Mayhew, Saleh, & Williams, 2016). As simple as this may seem, it is not an easy exercise to complete. An organisation must have the capacity to pinpoint its priorities, needs and challenges at any given time. When it comes to data particularly, the organisation must also have appropriate data to address the question. If the data are largely irrelevant to the question the organisation is trying to address, then how the data are gathered could be reshaped to address the question, which is an indispensable exercise to complete. If no data have been collected there is a need to implement data collection beforehand (see Batra, Jacobson, & Santhanam, 2015, on advanced analytics for instance).

Another important matter, also highlighted by Davenport, which is often lacking in data analytics processes across disciplines, is how to best interpret and disseminate the findings emerging from the data. This exercise requires a skill set in itself – more specifically, having a good understanding of what the organisation is trying to achieve, a general sense of business administration, and a capacity to be creative with analytics in order to identify patterns that may exist but are

When using big data to make big decisions, non-quants should focus on the first and the last steps of the process. The numbers people typically handle the details in the middle, but wise non-quants ask lots of questions along the way.	
1 Recognise the problem or question	Frame the decision or business problem and identify possible alternatives to the framing.
2 Review previous findings	Identify people who have tried to solve this problem (or similar ones) and the approaches they used.
3 Model the solution and select the variables	Formulate a detailed hypothesis about how particular variables affect the outcome.
4 Collect the data	Gather primary and secondary data on the hypothesised variables.
5 Analyse the data	Run a statistical model, assess its appropriateness for the data, and repeat the process until a good fit is found.
6 Present and act on the results	Use the data to tell a story to decision makers and stakeholders so that they will take action.

Figure 1.1 Decision-making process for analytics

Source: Adapted from Davenport (2013)

difficult to uncover in the first place; this skill set is scarce in reality. Performing data analytics needs to be understood as much more than clicking a few buttons with a program and looking at what comes out the other end of a computer. It requires curiosity, persistence, and a capacity to understand different possibilities the findings may be suggesting. Disseminating the findings to colleagues and clients is not necessarily an easy task either but must be equally emphasised otherwise all these efforts spent on data could essentially be worthless (Davenport, 2018). For analytics to benefit an organisation, the findings must be communicated clearly to the people in the organisation. The findings must be translated in a simple language so that people in the organisation can understand what these mean for them and for the organisation. The decision makers should also be clear on how to use the findings to implement a strategy that will benefit the organisation.

Importantly, being able to ask and answer appropriate questions, and to interpret and disseminate the findings, and to implement an organisational strategy based on data, all require a culture that will facilitate this process in the first place. For instance, the idea of 'culture catalysts' or analytics translators and support from decision makers in the organisation appears to be imperative if an organisation is seeking to be successful with an approach using evidence-based knowledge to benefit its needs. Underlying the culture and the challenges, a plan is needed to set up an approach driven by data from the organisation. The plan should match investment priorities with the organisational strategy, seek to balance the need for affordability and speed with business realities, and ensure frontline engagement and capabilities (see Biesdorf, Court, & Willmott, 2013).

The current context on big data in criminology and criminal justice

If organisational culture and the principles and processes underlying big data and data analytics are some of the key challenges for organisations in general, they are especially relevant for criminology and criminal justice. Criminology and criminal justice are largely considered applied disciplines where data collected through research are used, at least in theory, to inform policy and practical decisions (Lynch, 2018). The applied dimension of criminology typically involves the analysis of data in the form of case studies, prevalence rates, trends, and statistical associations for the purposes of informing law enforcement, the courts, and corrections as to evidence-based best practices. To these ends, both the discipline of criminology and the criminal justice systems that it seeks to inform have begun to integrate, to varying degrees, big data and data analytics. These are new developments in criminology, and undoubtedly are not being utilised to the same degree as in commercial contexts, such as long-standing practices of tailored advertisements for consumers (Simmons, 2016; Wall, 2018; Wigan & Clarke, 2013). Big data and data analytics in criminology and criminal justice, on the other hand, have seen comparatively limited application (see DeLisi, 2018), primarily in terms of surveillance (e.g., Miller, 2014), predicting the likelihood of recidivism (e.g., Wall, 2018), and in predictive policing applications (e.g., Brayne, 2017). Furthermore, the application of big data processes and analytics in criminal justice contexts is far from uniform; it varies across different legal jurisdictions, with some criminal justice organisations increasingly making use of big data and data analytics, and others more reluctant to do so, whether in law enforcement, the courts, or corrections (Koper, 2014). Indeed, the challenge of facilitating cultural shifts in organisational thinking in the criminal justice context is far from new and historically has more often than not been met with substantial resistance. Nonetheless, the proliferation of big data has led governments, alongside various components of the criminal justice system, to become increasingly interested in its potential applications.

In the criminal justice context, the appeal of big data reflects the culmination of relatively recent advances in technology, specifically in terms of the ubiquitous distribution of interconnected digital devices (Smith, Bennett Moses, & Chan, 2017), and the increasingly common practice of data-linkage. In terms of the former, a consequence of this interconnectivity is the constant generation and circulation of massive amounts of real-time data, which can range from locational data to metadata linked to online transactions (Kitchin, 2014). Data-linkage practices are becoming more common. They involve linking large administrative data sets from different government organisations and agencies with the key goal of better informing policy. Big data in criminology and criminal justice therefore primarily encapsulates both the massive data sets generated by interconnected devices and data-linkage, and the analytic techniques and tools that are employed to make sense of such large amounts of data (Chan, 2017). These characteristics set big data and the associated analytics apart from more traditional methods of data collection and statistical analysis in criminology, such as cross-sectional studies with specific samples and the use of survey instruments (Lynch, 2018). In terms of analysis, typical database software and analytic tools commonly used in criminology are increasingly becoming unable to capture, store, manage, and analyse the sheer volume of data and velocity with which it is generated. In other words, big data represents a new frontier for criminology and criminal justice, and in order to optimise the potential of generating positive outcomes and mitigating associated risks it is necessary to become forward thinking when it comes to adapting the tools, practices, and procedures of the trade accordingly, which is the focus of the current volume.

Despite its relatively recent appearance on the criminology and criminal justice landscapes, a healthy and robust debate about the implications of big data is emerging globally. To be sure, this is a positive development. At the same time, much of this is speculative and while interesting and thought-provoking, it is additionally necessary to advance the debate by generating empirical evidence about the application of big data and data analytics in criminology and criminal justice. For example, can big data and data analytics be used to determine if law enforcement patterns in a given community reflect over policing of certain sub-groups of the population? Skillicorn, Leuprecht, and Green investigate this very example in the case study of big data analytics and policing that they provide in Chapter 5. Some argue that the use of big data in criminology would shift analytic strategies from making inferences about populations based on specific samples, to analysing data encompassing the entire population (Bennett Moses & Chan, 2014; Chan & Bennett Moses, 2016). In the applied context of criminal justice, a key concern is that decision-making would shift away from individuals with 'expertise' and experience to data-driven decisions based on empirical patterns emerging out of big data (Bennett Moses & Chan, 2014; Simmons, 2016). Indeed, these concerns are not new in principle, one can look to the widespread use of, and controversies surrounding, actuarial risk assessment instruments in the context of corrections or sentencing grids to guide judicial decisions in different US states to name only a couple. Furthermore, what has emerged from the evidence along these lines is also not surprising; relying exclusively on either a large amount of data without any consideration of context, or vice versa, generalising from single and unique experiences to broader contexts does not typically produce accurate results or optimal outcomes in either scenario. These are some of the first 'fallacies' taught in undergraduate research methods courses; the ecological and exception fallacies. Nonetheless, given that the emergence of big data has advanced a shift toward a predictive approach to both knowledge and investigation in criminology and criminal justice (Mantelero & Vaciago, 2015), it seems that scholars with high quality research training are now more relevant than ever. In effect, emerging scholars trained in criminology might increasingly find themselves as 'culture catalysts' and/or 'analytics translators' in the era of big data and analytics when it comes to criminology and criminal justice.

Big data and criminology

The foregrounding of digital devices in day-to-day life is leading to the need for researchers to investigate digital data as not only a source of data itself, but also in terms of its impacts on criminal justice agencies and the public (Smith et al., 2017). Lee and Holt provide an in-depth discussion of the implications of this from a criminological perspective in Chapter 6. Indeed, the internet is the most prominent source of the digitisation of social life and has become so ubiquitous that criminological research can no longer afford to ignore it (Brewer, Cale, Goldsmith, & Holt, 2018). Big data processes and analytics in criminology will increasingly allow researchers to tap into new and emerging dimensions of social life and the data produced through these dimensions, such as the dynamic and real-time circulation of massive amounts of user-generated data that is enabled by the internet (Holt, Burruss, & Bossler, 2010; Williams, Burnap, & Sloan, 2017). Easily accessible dynamic and real-time sources of data also allow for the use of methods that are not retrospective compared to traditional criminological studies involving cross-sectional surveys or administrative data (Williams et al., 2017). Furthermore, the use of online sources for certain big data analytics also carries the distinction of being 'naturally occurring', and so for some criminological research questions, this potentially eliminates experimenter effects, or participant self-report and social desirability biases (Shah, Cappella, & Neuman, 2015).

While the transformative nature of big data has undoubtedly generated enthusiasm regarding the potential for criminological research, the implications, both positive and negative, need to be seriously considered. On the one hand, some have argued that the age of big data analytics represents the end of the scientific method (Anderson, 2008). For example, the first argument is that sampling would be rendered obsolete given the sheer volume of data available that would, in effect, encompass the entire population (Bennett Moses & Chan, 2014; Chan & Bennett Moses, 2016). The second argument is that massive volumes of data would lead to outliers and anomalies getting drowned out by more representative data points, allowing for insights despite the presence of errors (Bennett Moses & Chan, 2014). Finally, the third argument is that causality will no longer be a relevant factor because correlation would provide sufficient insight about the data (see Bennett Moses & Chan, 2014; Chan & Bennett Moses, 2016). For example, Miller (2014) argued that big data analytics circumvents the time-consuming experimental procedures of forming hypotheses, gathering data, and testing it; and that in a similar manner the use of computation to form correlations between data entities is simply more efficient than seeking causal explanations. Of course, this would come at the cost of eschewing a deeper understanding of the relationship between variables. This is a common problem in the context of data-linkage. These are interesting and contentious points; many including ourselves maintain that data by itself absent of context will always be meaningless and that researchers pursue data in response to specific questions that need to be answered, and furthermore, that are guided by theory. The necessity for understanding what issue or challenge organisations are trying to tap into must still be translated into an appropriate research question that can in fact be addressed by the data that are at hand. Furthermore, the same goes for criminal justice organisations; what is the organisation trying to address for its benefits? Is the goal to reduce returns to custody? Or is it to improve staff morale? In other words, what is the actual question that an organisation is seeking to answer? It seems Davenport's (2013) decision-making process discussed in the first section of the chapter has particular relevance for criminology and criminal justice in the era of big data and data analytics.

Big data and criminal justice

Big data also has clear implications for the day-to-day operations of the criminal justice system. Advancements in communications infrastructure have led to procedural changes in criminal justice processes such as collating information across separate surveillance systems (Brayne, 2017). Interpersonal and interactive communication between government agencies and the public via social media has provided an alternative to traditional news media. The use of big data in law enforcement and security intelligence contexts has been described as a change in the production of security; big data technology has been described as a power-amplifier that can enhance policing operations and technical expertise among individual police officers (Chan & Bennett Moses, 2017). Miller (2014) argued that big data has allowed for the creation of predictive systems that shift analytic focus from the individual to events. In effect, instead of surveillance being used to provide evidence against an identified suspect, one possibility is that surveillance might now be used to establish patterns from collected data which are then retroactively applied to individuals or groups in a predictive manner (Miller, 2014). The integration of such big data practices is highly controversial because it marks a turn from traditional discretion-based decision making to a more predictive approach based on empirical data (Simmons, 2016).

In the context of criminal justice, the empirical and analytic driven nature of big data conflicts with the long traditions of individual experience, training, intuition, and 'common sense' employed by criminal justice practitioners in making their decisions (Simmons, 2016). This challenge is not new; in many organisations, particularly criminal justice organisations, broad, flexible and imprecise standards for decision making and judgements (i.e., individual discretion) may be considered ideal because they allow for room to tailor decisions based on nuanced circumstances (Simmons, 2016). This remains the case, despite cognitive psychology literature suggesting that the use of data analytics involving a large amount of information, over intuition exclusively, can in fact improve human decision making (Hastie & Dawes, 2010). In the context of big data, however, the gulf between decision-making based on empirical evidence and individual discretion of criminal justice actors possibly widens substantially. Ferguson (2015) illustrated this through the example of the reasonable suspicion doctrine as enshrined in the Fourth Amendment of the US Constitution. Under this doctrine, police can only stop suspects if they have a reasonable suspicion based on the information about the individual that they know or based on the individual's activities that they observe. This means that suspicion falls on a particular individual at a particular time and place. On the other hand, big data allows officers to identify suspects through a database of personal information rather than through direct observations, allowing suspicion to be placed on multiple people who meet certain risk criteria (Ferguson, 2015). This important example raises two key questions.

The first is whether and to what extent individual officers would in fact rely on the data versus their own experience and intuition. A case study of the Los Angeles Police Department (Brayne, 2017) has described the use of predictive software and databases for a more proactive, predictive, and evidence-based form of policing, as a stark contrast with the traditional policing model of random patrols, rapid responses to 911 calls, and reactive investigations. Skillicorn et al. provide a demonstration of this in Chapter 5. However, the second paramount concern is whether and to what extent the data are biased through potentially discriminatory factors or variables that make up predictive algorithms based on the data (Simmons, 2016). Gerritsen provides an important discussion around these issues in Chapter 3. Clearly, big data has the potential to transform the criminal justice system and its processes, but it could be argued that its incompatibility with long-standing doctrines of discretion and individualised suspicion has meant that its impact on the workings of the criminal justice system to date has been limited compared to other contexts (Simmons, 2016; Wall, 2018; Wigan & Clarke, 2013).

The current volume

There are numerous ways to conceptualise and define big data, ranging from practical considerations of the hardware involved, to more abstract observations of its impact on individual behaviour and organisational policy. Whatever it may be, they all share the common characteristic of highlighting the transformative nature of big data. At the same time, big data and data analytics is not immune to errors; increased volume also means that there is greater potential for the impact mistakes have. Human biases will always be a factor in analytics, as it is a human researcher that identifies and selects which data to analyse and chooses which algorithms to use (see Gerritsen, Chapter 3). Another crucial consideration is that fact that as big data and data analytics and processes are adopted in the criminal justice context, so too are such processes being adopted by criminal elements (see Lee & Holt, Chapter 6). Both amateur and career criminals will utilise digital devices, infrastructures, and big data, not only to evade detection, but also to organise and execute criminal activity (Smith et al., 2017). Specifically, crimes may be conducted through the recording, analysis, visualisation, and use of digital data; and additionally, victimisation can occur or be experienced through the digital space as is the case for cybercrimes (Smith et al., 2017). With the aim of maintaining a forward-thinking approach as to how big data and data analytics can advance the field of criminology and the practice of criminal justice, this volume is divided into eight chapters.

Following the current introduction to the volume, in Chapter 2, DeLisi provides an important overview of the cultural divide between academic criminology and applied criminal justice and how big data can help to close this gap through an epidemiological lens. This aspect of Chapter 2 resonates strongly with the theme of culture discussed in the current chapter and some of the barriers that come along with it when it comes to engaging proactively with big data. Along these lines, DeLisi also discusses ways in which big data can be leveraged to improve public safety and criminal justice, with consideration toward some of the key obstacles that are faced and what some potential solutions may be.

Turning to Chapter 3, Gerritsen provides an explanation for how artificial intelligence (AI) techniques, such as machine learning and data mining, have been incorporated into criminal justice, and importantly, demystifies fact from much fiction that currently characterises many narratives surrounding AI. Gerritsen explains what in fact AI means in the context of criminal justice as well as the potential benefits and some case studies showcasing what the key issues around AI currently are when it comes to criminal justice. Her case studies reinforce a recent commentary by Dans (2019) that emphasises that digital transformation is as much if not more about an organisation's culture and people as it is about technological advancement.

In Chapter 4, Tayebi, Glässer, and Andresen further a related discussion around data mining and machine learning in the theoretical context of environmental criminology. Unlike some other theoretical traditions in criminology, environmental criminology is considered very much an 'applied' theoretical perspective. As Tayebi et al. explain, 'the field of environmental criminology is well-suited to the era of big data because of the types of data currently used in this research, but also because of the increased number of dimensions in the analyses considering both space and time'. Again, Tayebi et al. emphasise the importance of the nature of questions asked in research where big data and data analytics are employed in analyses, as well as the cultural consideration of working across academic disciplines in an interdisciplinary fashion in the era of big data.

In Chapter 5, Skillicorn, Leuprecht, and Green present an exploratory empirical study of the application of big data that investigates what can be learned from routine administrative data collected in police incident reports. Skillicorn et al. demonstrate the utility of routinely collected administrative data (in this case in the context of law enforcement) for not only identifying patterns in criminal activity that may promote intelligence led policing, but also how this data can be leveraged to improve service and enhance organisational excellence. In this exploratory analysis, they apply a novel analytic technique to an administrative law enforcement data set to examine whether or not there is evidence of bias in police service as well as what the data tell us about social networks identified in law enforcement data.

Lee and Holt turn the discussion in Chapter 6 toward how technological innovation has created unparalleled opportunities for crimes to evolve over the years. Further to this, they explain how the associated big data that is generated through online illegal activity can be leveraged by researchers to understand criminological phenomenon more fully. They discuss a wide range of cybercrimes and associated big data that provide enormous potential for criminological inquiry, as well as the challenges and dilemmas that accompany big data research in the criminological context.

In Chapter 7, Green discusses the complex relationship surrounding the implications of scientific advances in human genomics research on judicial processes in the criminal justice context, and how these are linked to modern large-scale bio-banking initiatives (i.e., big data). A key theme of this chapter underscores the complex relationship between behavioural research and how it translates into policy, particularly in the era of big data. Further elaborating this point, Green discusses the complex ethical dilemma posed by using what is essentially 'bio-banking' of genetic information for the purposes of criminal justice.

Finally, the volume concludes by highlighting some of the key themes to emerge across these chapters, followed by a proposed framework moving forward to facilitate engagement with big data and data analytics in the fields of criminology and criminal justice. The purpose of this is to facilitate engagement with big data and data analytics in proactive ways with an eye to understanding barriers and limitations and how to overcome them while at the same time ensuring the integrity and ethics of the knowledge generated through these means.

References

Anderson, C. (2008). The end of theory: The data deluge makes the scientific method obsolete. *Wired*. Retrieved from www.wired.com/2008/06/pb-theory/

Batra, G., Jacobson, Z., & Santhanam, N. (2015). Using the power of advanced analytics to improve manufacturing, R&D, and sales. *McKinsey on Semiconductors*, *5*, 68–78.

Bennett Moses, L., & Chan, J. (2014). Using big data for legal and law enforcement decisions: Testing the new tools. *University of New South Wales Law Journal*, *37*(2), 643–678.

Bernik, C. L. (2001, June). When your culture needs a makeover. *Harvard Business Review*, 53–61.

Biesdorf, S., Court, D., & Willmott, P. (2013, March). Big data: What's your plan? *McKinsey Quarterly*, 1–11.

Boudreau, J. W., & Ramstad, P. M. (2003). Strategic HRM measurement in the 21st century: From justifying HR to strategic talent leadership. In M. Goldsmith, R. P. Gandossy, & M. S. Efron (Eds.), *HRM in the 21st century* (pp. 79–90). New York: John Wiley.

Brayne, S. (2017). Big Data surveillance: The case of policing. *American Sociological Review*, *82*(5), 977–1008. https://doi.org/10.1177/0003122417725865

Brewer, R., Cale, J., Goldsmith, A., & Holt, T. (2018). Young people, the internet, and emerging pathways into criminality: A study of Australian adolescents. *International Journal of Cyber Criminology*, *12*, 115–132.

Chan, J. (2017, July 27). Big Data and visuality. *Oxford Research Encyclopedia of Criminology*. Retrieved from http://criminology.oxfordre.com/view/10.1093/acrefore/9780190264079.001.0001/acrefore-9780190264079-e-128

Chan, J., & Bennett Moses, L. (2016). Is big data challenging criminology? *Theoretical Criminology*, *20*(1), 21–39. https://doi.org/10.1177/1362480615586614

Chan, J., & Bennett Moses, L. (2017). Making sense of big data for security. *The British Journal of Criminology*, *57*(2), 299–319. https://doi.org/10.1093/bjc/azw059

Court, D. (2015, January). Getting big impact from Big Data. *McKinsey Quarterly*, 1–8.

Dans, E. (2019, March 21). Please, can we park the terminator hypothesis once and for all? *Forbes Magazine*. Forbes Media LLC. Retrieved from www.forbes.com/sites/enriquedans/2019/03/21/please-can-we-park-the-terminator-hypothesis-once-and-for-all/#140ca8913bc3

Davenport, T. H. (2013, July–August). Keep up with your quants. *Harvard Business Review*, 120–123.

Davenport, T. H. (2018). Data is worthless if you don't communicate it. In *Harvard Business Review guide to data analytics basics for managers* (pp. 173–176). Boston, MA: Harvard Business School Publishing Corporation.

Davenport, T. H., Harris, J., & Shapiro, J. (2010, October). Competing on talent analytics. *Harvard Business Review*, 52–58.

DeLisi, M. (2010). The big potential of epidemiological studies for criminology and forensics. *Journal of Forensic and Legal Medicine*, *57*, 24–27. https://doi.org/10.1016/j.jflm.2016.09.004

Diaz, A., Rowshankish, K., & Saleh, T. (2018, September). Why data culture matters? *McKinsey Quarterly*, 1–17.

Ferguson, A. G. (2015). Big data and predictive reasonable suspicion. *University of Pennsylvania Law Review*, *163*(2), 327–410.

Fleming, O., Fountaine, T., Henke, N., & Saleh, T. (2018). Ten red flags signaling your analytics program will fail. *McKinsey Analytics*, 1–9.

Groysberg, B., Lee, J., Price, J., & Yo-Jud Cheng, J. (2018, January–February). How to shape your culture. *Harvard Business Review*.

Hastie, R., & Dawes, R. M. (2010). *Rational choice in an uncertain world* (2nd ed.). Thousand Oaks, CA: Sage Publications.

Holt, T. J., Burruss, G. W., & Bossler, A. M. (2010). Social learning and cyber deviance: Examining the importance of a full social learning model in the virtual world. *Journal of Crime & Justice*, *33*, 31–62.

Kell, T., & Carrott, G. T. (2005, May). Culture matters most. *Harvard Business Review*.

Kitchin, R. (2014). Enablers and sources of big data. In R. Kitchin (Ed.), *The data revolution: Big data, open data, data infrastructures & their consequences* (pp. 80–99). London: SAGE Publications Ltd.

Koper, C. S. (2014). Assessing the practice of hot spots policing: Survey results from a national convenience sample of local police agencies. *Journal of Contemporary Criminal Justice*, *30*, 123–146. doi:10.1177/1043986214525079

Lawler, E. E., Levenson, A. R., & Boudreau, J. W. (2004). HR metrics and analytics: Use and impact. *Human Resource Planning Journal*, *27*, 27–35.

Lynch, J. (2018). Not even our own facts: Criminology in the era of Big Data. *Criminology*, *56*(3), 437–454. https://doi.org/10.1111/1745-9125.12182

Mantelero, A., & Vaciago, G. (2015). Data protection in a big data society: Ideas for a future regulation. *Digital Investigation*, *15*, 104–109.

Mayhew, H., Saleh, T., & Williams, S. (2016, October). Making data analytics work for you instead of the other way around. *McKinsey Quarterly*, 1–13.

McAfee, A., & Brynjolfsson, E. (2012, October). Big data: The management revolution. *Harvard Business Review*, 61–68.

Miller, K. (2014). Total surveillance, big data, and predictive crime technology: Privacy's perfect storm. *Journal of Technology Law & Policy*, *19*(1), 105–146.

Shah, D. V., Cappella, J. N., & Neuman, W. R. (2015). Big data, digital media, and computational social science: Possibilities and perils. *The Annals of the American Academy of Political and Social Science, 659*(1), 6–13.

Simmons, R. (2016). Quantifying criminal procedure: How to unlock the potential of big data in our criminal justice system. *Michigan State Law Review, 2016*(4), 947–1018.

Smith, G. J. D., Bennett Moses, L., & Chan, J. (2017). The challenges of doing criminology in the Big Data era: Towards a digital and data-driven approach. *The British Journal of Criminology, 57*(2), 259–274. https://doi.org/10.1093/bjc/azw096

Wall, D. (2018). How Big Data feeds big crime. *Current History, 117*(795), 29–34.

Wigan, M. R., & Clarke, R. (2013). Big Data's big unintended consequences. *Computer, 46*(6), 46–53. https://doi.org/10.1109/MC.2013.195

Williams, M. L., Burnap, P., & Sloan, L. (2017). Crime sensing with big data: The affordances and limitations of using open-source communications to estimate crime patterns. *The British Journal of Criminology, 57*(2), 320–340. https://doi.org/10.1093/bjc/azw031

2 The data are everywhere

Integrating criminology and epidemiology and improving criminal justice

Matt DeLisi

Introduction

Historically, the worlds of applied juvenile/criminal justice and academic criminology have for the most part been segregated. Many criminal justice practitioners perform their work duties without any connection to theory and research that exists in academic criminology. As a former practitioner who worked in the judicial sphere, the current author can attest to the sheer irrelevance of academia to applied criminal justice and the daily processing of criminal offenders. Even in more recent forays into various work relationships with local, state, and federal criminal justice organisations, the current author has witnessed that there is at best intermittent interest in academic knowledge on crime and justice among those that process and supervise criminal offenders. A reason for this disconnect is that academic criminologists are primarily interested in the theoretical, explanatory, or etiological reasons for why individuals engage in various forms of criminal behaviour. Scientific description and explanation are their job. In contrast, criminal justice professionals process offenders according to their violations of the criminal law, and the assorted reasons, rationales, or motivations for the criminal conduct are – even if intellectually interesting – not necessary to execute their work roles.

A similar relationship exists among most academic criminologists whose primary work duties are teaching and conducting and publishing research. Many studies are published from secondary data sources that are nearly ubiquitous (this concept is addressed often in this chapter) or from primary data collection from university students or other general population samples. It is more challenging to obtain data from active offenders or current correctional clients; thus, academic criminologists often do not try. There are many unfortunate consequences of the segregation of applied criminal justice and academic criminology primarily relating to the lost opportunities that come from a combined scholar-practitioner approach to crime. But another important unfortunate consequence relates to lost access to powerful and often rich data on criminal offenders and criminal justice processes.[1] Consider these introductory comments.

In every corner of the juvenile and criminal justice systems, there are informal and formal, unofficial and official types of data. In the world of policing, there are unofficial notes or tally sheets that include the names of juveniles, the reason the officer contacted the youth, and the officer's course of action upon contact, such as taking the child home, calling the youth's parents, transporting the youth to school or some other social service agency, or some other diversionary outcome. In the event the officer takes the youth into custody and thus effectively makes an arrest, there is an official record of this action. To continue with this example in the judicial and correctional spheres, the custody report is used to create a petition. If the prosecutor decides to move forward with the case, there is an adjudication hearing (or many) and in the event the youth is found guilty, he or she is adjudicated delinquent. At the disposition hearing, the sentence is meted out and can range from informal probation to commitment to a confinement facility. At every step of the way, whether the case is dismissed or continued through the justice system, there is a record of the event. There are data.

Fortunately, most adolescents do not engage in delinquent conduct with enough frequency or severity to draw the notice of law enforcement or the juvenile court. Among those adolescents that experience the aforementioned juvenile justice sequence, it is usually a one-off experience. But a minority of youth – approximately 10 percent or less – recurrently are contacted by police, placed in detention, petitioned and adjudicated, and are placed on probation, committed to training schools or confinement facilities, or placed on aftercare. For these recidivistic youth, it is not uncommon to have dozens and even hundreds of delinquent events, and these recidivistic youths are also those who are disproportionately responsible for the most violent offenses, including murder, sexual assaults, armed robberies, and aggravated assaults (DeLisi, 2005; Edelstein, 2016; Vaughn et al., 2011; Vaughn, Salas-Wright, DeLisi, & Maynard, 2014; Wolfgang, Figlio, & Sellin, 1972).

With some exceptions, the juvenile records of all offenders including the latter severe youth are sealed or expunged once the youth reaches the age of maturity. In terms of the criminal justice system, the process begins anew and even a young adult that has been contacted by the police dozens of times is in the eyes of the law viewed as a first-time arrestee. This is highly problematic in the sense that violent, recidivistic young offenders are given multiple opportunities to victimise others and revisit the justice process. If their juvenile delinquency data were made available and used to inform police and court decision-making, a more restrictive approach would likely be taken (Boland & Wilson, 1978), one that would forestall much victimisation.[2] In this way, lack of access to data places limitations on the crime control ability of the criminal justice system.

Current focus

The current chapter has three goals. First, the nascent area of big data research that has married criminology and criminal justice with epidemiology is examined with particular focus on studies that have used very large data sets to inform understanding of crime including ones that involve the current author's collaborative relationship with federal criminal justice practitioners. Beyond epidemiological studies, massive official data sources that exist for law enforcement, judicial, and correctional officers are also described. Second, the various ways that big data approaches to crime can improve public safety and enhance the criminal justice system are explored. Third, the assorted obstacles to big data within the criminal justice system and within the general public are examined along with potential solutions that would reduce these obstacles. An epidemiological approach to criminology is exceedingly broad and offers opportunities for interaction and exchange between the academic community and criminal justice practitioners that would further the scientific understanding of crime, especially among the most forensically rare offenders, and likely facilitate greater public safety.

Big data criminology

Epidemiology is the branch of medicine that quantifies the incidence, prevalence, and correlates of disease and other medical conditions. It relies on very large, population-based sources of data that include scores of measures of various medical symptoms, medical conditions, medication history, mental health symptoms, psychiatric diagnoses, personality symptoms and disorders, substance use, and – usually tangential to the purpose of the data collection – information on antisocial symptoms and behaviours. In many respects, the latter measures of antisocial behaviour were not variables of interest to the original investigators who collected the data, but instead were extraneous forms of data that are derivative of various psychiatric information (e.g., diagnosis for Conduct Disorder or Antisocial Personality Disorder). In this way, epidemiological data sets have ample data that is ripe to be analysed by scholars outside of epidemiology. The promise and recent application of epidemiological criminology in its various incarnations has been discussed previously (e.g., Akers & Lanier, 2009; Akers, Potter, & Hill, 2012; DeLisi, 2016; Lanier, Pack, & Akers, 2010).

A fundamental feature of epidemiological criminology is to mine epidemiological data sets for their behavioural data. Often, the panoramic nature of epidemiological data sources provides opportunities to have exponentially larger samples of offenders to study, which is particularly important when the subject matter of interest is rare or is constituted by offenders that are elusive to sample. This is particularly true in the event of the most violent and most psychiatrically disturbed offenders. For example, Vaughn, Salas-Wright, DeLisi, and Qian (2015) studied 1,226 individuals with antisocial personality disorder that had been sampled as part of the National Epidemiologic Survey on Alcohol and Related Conditions or NESARC. The NESARC is an epidemiological sample that contains data on 43,093 participants and includes scores of questions on alcohol and substance use disorders, psychiatric disorders, personality disorders, and a bevy of behavioural indicators. The NESARC, which has oversampled young adults between the ages of 18 and 24, Hispanics, and African Americans, has an exceptional response rate over 80 percent, and now has multiple waves of data to permit trend analyses.

In their study, Vaughn et al. (2015) found that about 70 percent of persons with antisocial personality disorder nevertheless managed adequate socioeconomic functioning and exhibited relatively little evidence of intergenerational conti-nuity in antisocial conduct, that is, their children and/or parents were not also affected by the disorder. In contrast, about 9.4 percent of persons with antisocial personality disorder had parents or children with conduct problems and 20.3 percent of those with antisocial personality disorder exhibited multigenerational family histories of problem behaviours spanning grandfather to father to son. The latter group was characterised by clinical and personality disorders, alco-hol abuse, versatile criminal behaviours, and diverse acts of physical violence. Given the nature of antisocial personality disorder, it is generally believed that all affected individuals will require considerable social supports given their likelihood of involvement in crime. However, the big data investigation found that surprisingly, most individuals with antisocial personality disorder neverthe-less are able to achieve a modicum of conventional, prosocial functioning. In this way, prevention programs should target antisocial individuals for whom crime runs in their family in order to potentially effectuate the greatest potential crime reduction.

Overwhelmingly, big data is aptly named because of the massive size of the sample and its geographic scope. Sometimes, however, big data relates less to sample size and more to the breadth and depth of the data at hand. To illustrate, the current author has an ongoing research collaboration with United States Probation and Pretrial Services, the organisation that supervises clients that have been con-victed of federal crimes and placed on various sentences including probation and supervised release after a commitment to the Bureau of Prisons. This relationship has resulted in access to the entire supervision population within a federal juris-diction and also access to a 5-year census of persons that had ever been arrested for a sexual offense. The following study relates to the latter data source.

A common federal crime for which offenders are convicted and supervised is possession of child pornography. These offenders receive extensive treatment while on supervision and one facet of this treatment involves polygraphed inter-views where the defendant reveals his or her sexual history including instances of sexual violence. These are the type of 'hidden' data that usually are never encountered by academic criminologists. Fortunately, the current author was able to access them and in a recent study (DeLisi et al., 2016), found that 69 percent of sex offenders, many of whom were convicted of non-contact offenses, divulged a hands-on, contact victim during their criminal career. In addition, 34 offenders had zero official contacts for sexual offenses but reported sexual crimes against 148 victims an average of more than four victims per offender. The substantive importance of this finding is difficult to overstate. These are sexual victimisations that were previously unknown to supervising officers, and upon their discov-ery, could be used to facilitate a more stringent containment approach (English, Jones, Patrick, & Pasini-Hill, 2003) to supervising offenders that might appear lower-risk on paper, but much higher risk when considering all available data. In other words, criminological study of a correctional population produced data and research findings that directly translated into applied practice regarding the accurate risk assessment and supervision of sexual offenders.

Even the largest epidemiological data set is often entirely lacking the most severe types of criminal offenders that engage in the most serious forms of violence. In the United States, there are data sources that are truly massive, but these are almost entirely outside the purview of the research community (this is addressed in the obstacles and solutions section). For example, the Interstate Identification Index (III) is a finger-print based data source on offenders that have been arrested in the United States. Inquiries for criminal history information are made through the automated National Crime Information Center (NCIC) telecommunication system that is maintained by the Federal Bureau of Investigation. How this works in practice is that an offender's name and date of birth are entered into the computer, and within seconds, the state and/or FBI identification numbers are sent which can then be used to search, access, and print criminal history information. The NCIC contains seven property files and 14 person files including those on supervised release, the National Sex Offender Registry, foreign fugitives, immigration violators, missing persons, protection orders, unidentified persons, protective interest, gang members, known or appropriately suspected terrorists, wanted persons, identity theft, violent person, and National Instant Criminal Background Check System (NICS) Denied Transactions (Federal Bureau of Investigation, 2018). NCIC and III contain criminal history files for 110,235,200 persons of which all are automated with the exception of 4,307,500 manual records (Goggins & DeBacco, 2018). More than six million criminal history inquiries have been made on a single day and the average response time using the NCIC is a mere 0.06 seconds!

That criminal justice practitioners have instantaneous access to III and NCIC records is critically important in helping law enforcement, judicial, and correctional officers perform their duties. But the more than 110 million cases of offender data, including persons who have perpetrated serial homicides, rapes, or child molestation, cannot be touched by academics and even some criminal justice practitioners. Imagine the promise of such data to the research community particularly researchers that are embedded within criminal justice organisations and that work with offenders.

Big data informing criminal justice and enhancing public safety

Not all official criminal justice system data are off limits to the research community; indeed some data are made instantly available to the general public. This is especially true in circumstances that involve child victims. Unfortunately, homicides involving child victims commonly serve as the impetus for major innovations in the criminal justice system. For instance, the 1996 kidnapping and murder of 9-year-old Amber Hagerman (a case that has never been solved) resulted in the creation of the America's Missing Broadcast Emergency Response Alert system or AMBER Alert system. AMBER Alerts involve emergency notification in the event of an abducted child, and this includes information about the child, potential suspects in the abduction, and the abductor's vehicle description. This information is sent to mobile phones by text, appears on public radio stations, and is presented on video screens, traffic displays, and billboards along inter-states. In short, AMBER Alerts are a rapid dissemination of data to the public to exponentially increase the number of persons that can potentially make a visual identification of the victim and/or suspect. In the parlance of routine activities theory (Cohen & Felson, 1979), AMBER Alerts make nearly everyone a capable guardian.

Curiously, AMBER Alerts have been criticised by criminologists on the grounds that the policy is more symbolic than practically effective and for the notion that the alerts minimise the reality that most abductions are by family members and not homicidal strangers (see Griffin, 2010; Griffin & Miller, 2008; Miller, Alvarez, & Weaver, 2018). To be frank, criminologists tend to conde-scendingly and dismissively view AMBER Alerts as part of 'crime control the-ater'. Interestingly, their own data reject such minimisation. For instance, Griffin's (2010) study of 333 AMBER Alert successful cases found that in 51.6 percent of them, a citizen tip led to the recovery of the abducted child. In 20.5 percent of cases, the alert induced the offender to release the child victim and surrender. These are very successful outcomes. The potential criminal threat of abductors is also not trivial. In 22.6 percent of cases, the offender used or threatened to use lethal force and in 34.2 percent of cases the offender used or threatened to use non-lethal force. In 83.7 percent of cases, the abductor is a family member or acquaintance and in 16.3 percent of cases the abductor is a stranger (in 5.3 percent of cases the abductor is a known sex offender). Thus, although most child abductions are family squabbles, it does not mean that the family member is necessarily less of a physical threat to the child than a stranger would be.

The delay between abduction and recovery in AMBER Alert success stories is on average just 15.2 hours. The rapid dissemination of data creates alert and sometime hyper-vigilant observers among the general public. In Griffin's study, 19.5 percent of cases were resolved in three hours or less. In 44.2 percent of cases, the child was safely returned between three to twelve hours later. In nearly 86 percent of cases, the child was safely returned within 24 hours of their abduction. The rapidity of the safe return of abducted children shows the promise of massive dissemination of crime data accessible on one's phone.

In the wake of other high-profile abduction, rape, and murder of child vic-tims, the United States initiated a concerted effort to notify the public of the res-idency and terms of supervision of sexual offenders. Two of the most prominent legislative acts are the Adam Walsh Child Protection and Safety Act of 2006 and the Jacob Wetterling Crimes Against Children and Sex Offender Registration Act of 1994 (both Walsh and Wetterling were murdered by paedophilic sexual homicide offenders). The resulting creation and proliferation of sex offender registries is a clear example where big data on correctional clients are made available to the general public. The effectiveness of sexual offender registration and notification is unclear with some studies showing the policies are effective at identifying sex offender that recidivate (Jennings & Zgoba, 2015; Letourneau & Armstrong, 2008), while others have found limited effectiveness (Chaffin, 2008; Zgoba et al., 2016).[3]

Of course, there is always room for improvement. For instance, studies of recidivism of sex offenders have found that those identified as the lowest risk according to the Walsh Act had higher recidivism for sexual and non-sexual crimes than sex offenders that were classified as moderate or high risk (Freeman & Sandler, 2010; Zgoba et al., 2016). Even if sex offender registries are controversial vis-à-vis their ability to identify the offenders that are most likely to recidivate, that is ultimately a criminological question. Of more practical importance is that sex offender registries exist so that parents and other concerned citizens can utilise the data to make informed decisions relating to where they live, where they recreate, and where they work. The Hagerman, Walsh, and Wetterling families would certainly have appreciated having access to such data.

Big data obstacles and solutions

Having access to data is one matter, using it is another. Despite the ubiquity of data on sex offender registries, there are basic problems that relate not only to the usefulness of the data, but also to the willingness or interest of the general public to consume the data. Studies have shown, for example, that the few people in the general public actually use sex offender registries because of basic lack of interest, due to perceptions that their community is safe and thus likely does not have a sex offender presence, or because citizens do not have children and thus feel little sense of vulnerability or risk (Anderson & Sample, 2008; Kernsmith, Comartin, Craun, & Kernsmith, 2009). Others have also shown apathy and lack of knowledge among the public about sex offender registries and notification efforts (Levenson, Brannon, Fortney, & Baker, 2007). To be blunt, the general public generally does not care about criminal justice data, big or otherwise.

Sex offender registries are not the only form of criminal justice data that are available to the general public. Most county jail rosters and state departments of corrections have extensive websites that provide the current roster of inmates in the case of jails and fully searchable databases of inmates and correctional clients in the case of state-level sites. Again, it is likely that most citizens are not aware of these data resources, likely for a variety of reasons, including apathy and disinterest, lack of application to their daily life, and limited victimisation experiences and associated fear of crime.

The current author proposes two solutions to boost the lack of interest in big correctional data. First, criminologists should use websites of criminal justice data in their classes to provide exposure and instruction on how to use the sites and the types of information they provide. For instance, showing the local jail roster provides insight into the types of charges that jail inmates have, demographic characteristics of jail inmates, data on bond, correctional holds, state statutes, and other information. The current author can personally attest to the popularity of using local jail data to inform classroom lecture and instruction and understand social processes that affect crime, such as the clustering of arrests for public intoxication and other alcohol violations on the day of college football games. Similar, the use of local sex offender registries allows students the opportunity to search these websites and examine the number of registered sex offenders that live in close proximity to them. Anecdotally, most undergraduates have admitted to me that they have never used sex offender registries. The large exception to that are students who are also parents.

Second, criminologists should take advantage of online official criminal justice data for research purposes. Again, the current author has used online correctional data to conduct studies of institutional misconduct (DeLisi, 2003) and violent criminals (DeLisi, Beauregard, & Mosley, 2017). The latter study is particularly important since it covers exceedingly violent offenders that are unlikely to be found in general population and student samples. In fact, it is probably impossible to find armed burglary offenders in the general population using conventional sampling approaches. Accessing data thus facilitates important teaching and research endeavours and permits inclusion of rare, forensically fascinating offenders that academics would otherwise never contact.

The epidemiological scope of III and NCIC data is unparalleled, unfortunately almost no one can access these data especially for research purposes. The Federal Bureau of Investigation has a memorandum of understanding that prohibits the use of NCIC data for research purposes. Currently, only the Bureau of Justice Statistics, United States Sentencing Commission, and Administrative Office of the US Courts Probation and Pretrial Services are able to access NCIC and III data to assess recidivism outcomes for persons under or formerly under federal supervision. This means that local and state law enforcement, county sheriffs, state and federal probation, state parole, and other criminal justice organisations cannot use these data for research even though these organisations can use the NCIC for law enforcement and other specific judicial or correctional tasks. At the very least, criminal justice organisations should be able to access III and NCIC data to conduct research that is consistent with the function of their organisation, such as risk assessment with follow-up of recidivism data. In the event that academic criminologists have associations with criminal justice organisations, III and NCIC access should also be provided. Greater data access could result in new insights into offender behaviour and the development of better risk assessment actuarial tools which in turn could enhance the effectiveness of the justice system and potential bolster public safety.

Another data source that is epidemiological in scope is sexual assault kits (SAKs), which is a forensic medical exam that is conducted on the victims of sexual assault.[4] According to a recent summary review on the national problem of untested SAKs (Campbell, Feeney, Fehler-Cabral, Shaw, & Horsford, 2017), there are more than 200,000 untested SAKs in the United States. SAKs are not routinely submitted for DNA testing for a variety of reasons including lack of victim consent or release of their SAK to be tested, financial limitations that law enforcement and county attorney offices have to DNA test the kits in a timely manner, perceived utility of DNA testing for the investigation, and other reasons. Regardless of the reason, that so many untested SAKs sit on shelves in evidence rooms in the United States is an appalling disservice to victims of sexual violence and a fundamental affront to crime control and due process.

Fortunately, many jurisdictions are working to change the conversation on untested SAKs toward the realisation of justice. For instance, the Cuyahoga County (Cleveland, Ohio) SAK Task Force tested approximately 5,000 SAKs in its jurisdiction in part using a grant from the Cuyahoga County Prosecutor's Office. In turn, academics at Case Western Reserve University obtained grant funding from the United States Bureau of Justice Assistance to analyse the SAK data (Lovell et al., 2017). Their research findings were critically important. Of the 433 SAKs in their sample, 56.3 percent were connected to serial sexual offenders. Compared to non-serial sexual offenders, serial sexual offenders were significantly more likely to rape strangers, to kidnap their victim, to perpetrate sexual assault while using or displaying a firearm or knife, and to employ verbal threats and physical abuse of their victim. Increasing the number of SAKs that are tested and analysed thus offers considerable opportunities for identifying sexual aggressors for arrest, prosecution, and incapacitation.

Conclusion

Crime and criminal justice data are everywhere, particularly if one knows where to look. The ubiquity of these data renders them broader than any epidemiological data collection effort one could ever hope to accomplish. But these data are often under-utilised and at times prohibited for counterproductive, bureaucratic reasons (e.g., III and NCIC data). The general public is already aware of big data in the event of AMBER Alerts, and to a lesser degree sex offender registries, but more investment on the part of the public is needed for these data to reach their fullest potential. Finally, the historically segregated worlds of academic criminology and applied criminal justice continue, but there are powerful illustrations of the promise of a collaborative, scholar-practitioner approach to crime, such as focused deterrence programs in law enforcement and the current author's work with federal sex offenders. More criminologists should get their hands dirty with real offenders and work along with criminal justice practitioners to take advantage of data of unparalleled depth and richness.

Notes

1 There are also ideological and cultural differences between applied criminal justice and academic criminology, and as such, professional turf squabbles between the two. The diverse issues that exist between criminal justice practitioners and academic criminologists and thus the distortions that have arisen have been recently described (see Wright & DeLisi, 2017). Unfortunately, this has likely resulted in the irrelevancy of criminology to the administration of justice. Consider Braga and Apel's (2016, p. 825, italics added for emphasis) recent commentary on this issue: 'Considerable scientific evidence and practical experience can support an informed opinion on how the police should be deployed to control crime in cities. The public certainly deserves better than an unfocused suggestion to halt potentially helpful police innovations and wait for academics to complete a definitive study of the relationship between perceived and actual sanction risks. *And we wonder why criminology is sometimes considered irrelevant in real-world policy conversations*'.

2 In practice, juvenile delinquent histories are used in the criminal justice system particularly in cases where an adult offender continues to accumulate arrest activity in the same jurisdiction where he or she accrued juvenile history. In this scenario, criminal justice practitioners are not circumventing the law, but instead merely remember prior instances when they interacted with the offender in a policing, judicial, or correctional capacity. To illustrate, the current author interviewed some defendants more than 20 times during his tenure as a pretrial services officer, which speaks to the chronicity with which some offenders are arrested and the considerable institutional memory that exists within the criminal justice system about specific offenders.

3 A substantive reason for disparate findings is that sexual offenders are highly heterogeneous in terms of the duration of their criminal career, the degree with which they specialise in sexual crimes or generalise to other forms of crime, and the prevalence of severe psychopathology, especially sexual sadism and psychopathy (see Cale et al., 2015; Cale et al., 2016; Lussier & Cale, 2013).

4 The forensic medical exam for an SAK is itself a sensitive and invasive procedure that involves the collection of photographs of the victim's injuries, head and pubic hair, fingernail scrapings, and swabs of bodily orifices and other bodily areas to collect semen, blood, and saliva (see Campbell et al., 2017). Given the extremely sensitive nature of these data, it is understood that there would be opposition to releasing these data for research purposes.

References

Adam Walsh Child Protection and Safety Act of 2006, 109 U.S.C. § 4472.

Akers, T. A., & Lanier, M. M. (2009). "Epidemiological criminology": Coming full circle. *American Journal of Public Health, 99*(3), 397–402. doi:10.2105/AJPH.2008.139808

Akers, T. A., Potter, R. H., & Hill, C. V. (2012). *Epidemiological criminology: A public health approach to crime and violence*. Hoboken, NJ: John Wiley & Sons.

Anderson, A. L., & Sample, L. L. (2008). Public awareness and action resulting from sex offender community notification laws. *Criminal Justice Policy Review, 19*(4), 371–396. https://doi.org/10.1177/0887403408316705

Boland, B., & Wilson, J. Q. (1978). Age, crime, and punishment. *The Public Interest, 51,* 22-34.

Braga, A. A., & Apel, R. (2016). And we wonder why criminology is sometimes considered irrelevant in real-world policy conversations. *Criminology & Public Policy, 15*(3), 813–829. doi:10.1111/1745-9133.12235

Cale, J., Lussier, P., McCuish, E., & Corrado, R. (2015). The prevalence of psychopathic personality disturbances among incarcerated youth: Comparing serious, chronic, violent and sex offenders. *Journal of Criminal Justice, 43*(4), 337–344. https://doi.org/10.1016/j.crimjus.2015.04.005

Cale, J., Smallbone, S., Rayment-McHugh, S., & Dowling, C. (2016). Offense trajectories, the unfolding of sexual and non-sexual criminal activity, and sex offense characteristics of adolescent sex offenders. *Sexual Abuse: A Journal of Research and Treatment, 28*(8), 791–812. doi:10.1177/1079063215580968

Campbell, R., Feeney, H., Fehler-Cabral, G., Shaw, J., & Horsford, S. (2017). The national problem of untested sexual assault kits (SAKs): Scope, causes, and future directions for research, policy, and practice. *Trauma, Violence, & Abuse, 18*(4), 363–376. doi:10.1177/1524838015622436

Chaffin, M. (2008). Our minds are made up: Don't confuse us with the facts: Commentary on policies concerning children with sexual behavior problems and juvenile sex offenders. *Child Maltreatment, 13*(2), 110–121. doi:10.1177/1077559508314510

Cohen, L. E., & Felson, M. (1979). Social change and crime rate trends: A routine activity approach. *American Sociological Review, 44*(4), 588–608. doi:10.2307/2094589

DeLisi, M. (2003). Criminal careers behind bars. *Behavioral Sciences & the Law, 21*(5), 653–669. doi:10.1002/bsl.531

DeLisi, M. (2005). *Career criminals in society.* Thousand Oaks, CA: Sage.

DeLisi, M. (2016). The big data potential of epidemiological studies for criminology and forensics. *Journal of Forensic and Legal Medicine.* https://doi.org/10.1016/j.flm.2016.09.004

DeLisi, M., Beauregard, E., & Mosley, H. (2017). Armed burglary: A marker for extreme instrumental violence. *Journal of Criminal Psychology, 7*(1), 3–12. https://doi.org/10.1108/JCP-08-2016-0023

DeLisi, M., Caropreso, D. E., Drury, A. J., Elbert, M. J., Evans, J. L., Heinrichs, T., & Tahja, K. (2016). The dark figure of sexual offending: New evidence from federal sex offenders. *Journal of Criminal Psychology, 6*(1), 3–15. https://doi.org/10.1108/JCP-12-2015-0030

Edelstein, A. (2016). Rethinking conceptual definitions of the criminal career and serial criminality. *Trauma, Violence, & Abuse, 17*(1), 62–71. https://doi.org/10.1177/152483 8014566694

English, K., Jones, L., Patrick, D., & Pasini-Hill, D. (2003). Sexual offender containment: Use of the postconviction polygraph. *Annals of the New York Academy of Sciences, 989*(1), 411–427. doi:10.1111/j.1749-6632.2003.tb07322.x

Federal Bureau of Investigation. (2018). National Crime Information Center (NCIC). Retrieved February 9, 2018 from www.fbi.gov/services/cjis/ncic

Freeman, N. J., & Sandler, J. C. (2010). The Adam Walsh Act: A false sense of security or an effective public policy initiative? *Criminal Justice Policy Review, 21*(1), 31–49. https://doi.org/10.1177/088740340933565

Goggins, B. R., & DeBacco, D. A. (2018). *Survey of state criminal history information systems, 2016: A criminal justice information policy report.* Washington, DC: U.S. Department of Justice, Office of Justice Programs and Bureau of Justice Statistics.

Griffin, T. (2010). An empirical examination of AMBER Alert "successes". *Journal of Criminal Justice, 38*(5), 1053–1062. doi:10.1016/j.jcrimjus.2010.07.008

Griffin, T., & Miller, M. K. (2008). Child abduction, AMBER Alert, and crime control theater. *Criminal Justice Review, 33*(2), 159–176. doi:10.1177/0734016808316778

The Jacob Wetterling Crimes against Children and Sex Offender Registration Act, 42 U.S.C. § 14071 (1994).

Jennings, W. G., & Zgoba, K. M. (2015). An application of an innovative cost-benefit analysis tool for determining the implementation costs and public safety benefits of SORNA with educational implications for criminology and criminal justice. *Journal of Criminal Justice Education, 26*(2), 147–162. https://doi.org/10.1080/10511253.2014.940057

Kernsmith, P. D., Comartin, E., Craun, S. W., & Kernsmith, R. M. (2009). The relationship between sex offender registry utilization and awareness. *Sexual Abuse: A Journal of Research and Treatment, 21*(2), 181–193. https://doi.org/10.1177/1079063209332235

Lanier, M. M., Pack, R. P., & Akers, T. A. (2010). Epidemiological criminology: Drug use among African American gang members. *Journal of Correctional Health Care, 16*(1), 6–16. doi:10.1177/1078345809348199

Letourneau, E. J., & Armstrong, K. S. (2008). Recidivism rates for registered and nonregistered juvenile sexual offenders. *Sexual Abuse: A Journal of Research and Treatment, 20*(4), 393–408. doi:10.1177/1079063208324661

Levenson, J. S., Brannon, Y. N., Fortney, T., & Baker, J. (2007). Public perceptions about sex offenders and community protection policies. *Analyses of Social Issues and Public Policy, 7*(1), 137–161. doi:10.1111/j.1530-2415.2007.00119.x

Lovell, R., Luminais, M., Flannery, D. J., Overman, L., Huang, D., Walker, T., & Clark, D. R. (2017). Offending patterns for serial sex offenders identified via the DNA testing of previously unsubmitted sexual assault kits. *Journal of Criminal Justice, 52*, 68–78. http://dx.doi.org/10.1016/j.crimjus.2017.08.002

Lussier, P., & Cale, J. (2013). Beyond sexual recidivism: A review of the sexual criminal career parameters of adult sex offenders. *Aggression and Violent Behavior, 18*(5), 445–457. doi:10.1016/j.avb.2013.06.005

Miller, M. K., Alvarez, M. J., & Weaver, J. (2018). Empirical evidence for AMBER Alert as crime control theater: A comparison of student and community samples. *Psychology, Crime & Law, 24*(2), 83–104. doi:10.1080/1068316X.2017.1390572

Vaughn, M. G., DeLisi, M., Gunter, T., Fu, Q., Beaver, K. M., Perron, B. E., & Howard, M. O. (2011). The severe 5%: A latent class analysis of the externalizing behavior spectrum in the United States. *Journal of Criminal Justice, 39*(1), 75–80. https://doi.org/10.1016/j.crimjus.2010.12.001

Vaughn, M. G., Salas-Wright, C. P., DeLisi, M., & Maynard, B. R. (2014). Violence and externalizing behavior among youth in the United States: Is there a severe 5%? *Youth Violence and Juvenile Justice, 12*(1), 3–21. https://doi.org/10.1177/1541204013478973

Vaughn, M. G., Salas-Wright, C. P., DeLisi, M., & Qian, Z. (2015). The antisocial family tree: Family histories of behavior problems in antisocial personality in the United States. *Social Psychiatry and Psychiatric Epidemiology, 50*(5), 821–831. https://doi.org/10.1007/s00127-014-0987-9

Wolfgang, M. E., Figlio, R. M., & Sellin, T. (1972). *Delinquency in a birth cohort*. Chicago, IL: University of Chicago Press.

Wright, J. W., & DeLisi, M. (2017). What criminologists don't say, and why. *City Journal, 27*(3), 50–57.

Zgoba, K. M., Miner, M., Levenson, J., Knight, R., Letourneau, E., & Thornton, D. (2016). The Adam Walsh Act: An examination of sex offender risk classification systems. *Sexual Abuse: A Journal of Research and Treatment, 28*(8), 722–740. doi:10.1177/1079063215569543

3 Big data and criminology from an AI perspective

Charlotte Gerritsen

Introduction

In modern society much data is gathered even without us being aware of it. Cameras record our every movement while walking through a shopping mall, cookies track our browsing behaviour, and customer service cards keep track of our habits while buying groceries. All of this is done with a reason: the end users of the tracking device want to get to know its users to, for example, ensure tailored ads or optimise profits. In modern digital society the possibilities of using large data sets are endless, but while gathering data is relatively simple using such large amounts of data in a meaningful manner is a bit more complicated.

Once the data have been collected they need to be analysed for a specific purpose. Because of the constant growth of these ever-expanding data sets, which are commonly referred to as *big data*, they cannot be analysed manually with traditional statistical methods since these data sets have outgrown those possibilities. However, large data sets can be analysed rather efficiently using computational methods.

In this chapter I will go into the potential of big data in the field of criminology, with an emphasis on the discipline that provides the algorithms that are needed to process such large amounts of data: artificial intelligence (AI). I will first explain the different techniques that are used while analysing big data sets. Next, I will provide an overview of existing projects that use big data to predict crime. I will conclude with the pros and cons of the use of AI techniques in the field of criminology and discuss the possibilities of AI in future criminological research.

Big data and artificial intelligence

To analyse big data, data science techniques are applied (Figure 3.1). In this section I will explain the methods of *machine learning* and *data mining*. I will explain what the difference between these methods is and how they can be applied in criminological research.

Machine learning

Machine learning (ML) is the research area that aims to make a computer system learn intelligent behaviour from data, which has not been programmed in advance

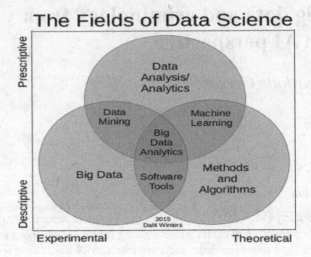

The Fields of Data Science

Figure 3.1 The fields of data science
Source: Dahl Winters (2015)[1]

(Samuel, 1959). Different algorithms are explored that can learn from data and can make predictions (Kohavi & Provost, 1998). These algorithms use sample inputs to construct a model to make data-driven predictions or decisions (Bishop, 2006). Typically, a large part of a data set is used as training set to make the system learn. After the learning process it can be used to make *predictions* based on other data. ML is employed in a range of computing tasks where designing and programming explicit algorithms with good performance is difficult or infeasible. Within the criminological domain, this method has, among others, been used in drug related crime research in Taiwan (Lin, Chen, & Yu, 2017) and in estimating the risk in recidivism (Siegel, 2013).

Data mining

Data mining and ML use the same methods but have a different focus. Data mining is defined as the practice of examining large pre-existing databases in order to generate new information (Friedman, 1998). While ML focuses on prediction, based on *known* properties learned from the training data, data mining focuses on the discovery of *unknown* properties in the data. In ML, performance is usually evaluated with respect to the ability to *reproduce known* knowledge, while in data mining the key task is the discovery of previously *unknown* knowledge. Examples of criminological research in which data mining is used are credit card fraud (Bhattacharyya, Jha, Tharakunnel, & Westland, 2011) cybercrime (Chen et al., 2004), and drug trafficking (Chiranjeevi & Revathy, 2015).

Sentiment analysis is a specific form of data mining in which the level of sentiment in large data sets is analysed (Pang & Lee, 2008). Different techniques are combined (e.g., natural language processing, biometrics, and computational linguistics) in order to systematically identify, extract, quantify, and study affective states and subjective information. Sentiment analysis is used to determine the emotional state of the text. Sentiment analysis can be used for, among other things, determining the emotion in large crowds to predict the dynamics of the mass, for example, in case of a sporting event, festival, or demonstration (Gerritsen & Van Breda, 2015) or to predict crime locations (Gerber, 2014) by analysing social media feed.

AI in criminology

While big data can be gathered for many different purposes, criminology is one of the research areas in which it can have particularly profound impact (Chen et al., 2003; McClendon & Meghanathan, 2015). Using big data sets in criminology provides great opportunities. For example, one area in which the use of big data currently flourishes is in the field of predictive policing. Predictive policing refers to the usage of mathematical, predictive, and analytical techniques in law enforcement to identify potential criminal activity (Rienks, 2015). Four categories can be distinguished in the field of predictive policing, namely methods for predicting 1) crimes, 2) offenders, 3) perpetrators' identities, and 4) victims of crime (Perry & McInnis, 2013). Predictions are made based on large data sets, making predictive policing a nice illustration of ML.

Case studies

There exist many applications in which big data is used to make predictions in crime-related areas. Some of these applications are fiction, although they might borderline reality, and others are actually in practice or are being developed as we speak. In this section I want to highlight some of these applications to illustrate the potential of big data in criminological research. I will first start with two fictional examples. Although the examples are a figment of the imagination of the director, they nicely illustrate the potential of predictive systems in the field of crime.

Fiction

Minority Report

In 2002 Steven Spielberg directed the movie *Minority Report* (based on the short story written by Philip K. Dick in 1956). In this movie, based in 2054, a special police unit ('Precrime') is able to predict future crimes. The system that predicts these crimes is based on three gifted humans with special powers that can see into the future and predict crimes beforehand. While the main topic of the movie is free will and determinism, the movie illustrates quite nicely what the consequences might be when using a predictive system. In the movie the head of the police unit is predicted to become a murderer. While his colleagues start to chase him, he believes this prediction is a flaw of the system. This illustrates the biggest fear people have while using predictive systems; the system might be wrong. How do you want to use a system? Can you let a system operate autonomously, without any human interference? Next to that, in the movie people get arrested based on the predictions of the system. Can you punish people for something they have not yet done but are expected to do in the future? These questions lead to an interesting discussion on the potential use of future crime prediction systems like the one in *Minority Report*.

Persons of Interest

While *Minority Report* was labelled sci-fi in 2002, the 2011 TV series *Persons of Interest* was labelled 'action/crime', perhaps indicating that this topic might not be that farfetched anymore. In this series a software genius creates a machine for the government to detect acts of terror before they can happen by monitoring the entire world through every cell phone, email, and surveillance camera. The machine is able to see everything from terrorist acts to violent crimes. When the government considered violent crimes between normal people out of their scope of interest, the creator built a back door into the system that gives him the social security number of a person involved in a future violent crime so he could act and prevent violent crimes before they can happen.

   Although the examples mentioned here are fictional, today systems with similar intentions actually exist and are in fact used on daily base. The underlying purpose of these systems is to predict where crime will happen. In the following section I will highlight a number of these systems.

Reality

Crime Anticipation System

The Amsterdam Police force developed the Crime Anticipation System (CAS)[2] to predict high impact crimes (e.g., robbery, burglary). In this system, the city of Amsterdam is divided into squares of 125 x 125 meters. Locations less likely to attract crime (e.g., open water, fields) are discarded. For all the other squares, data are gathered like historic crime incidents, distance to known suspects, distance to highways, number and types of businesses present, demographic, and socio-economic information of the population. Based on this information CAS predicts the likelihood of an incident in the coming two weeks. Locations with a high probability are marked as a 'high-risk' area. These areas need more attention and can be monitored more frequently. Some suggest that CAS is currently able to successfully predict a substantial proportion of burglaries and robberies.[3]

PredPol

The Los Angeles Police Department and UCLA joined forces in the development of PredPol,[4] with the goal of investigating whether existing data sets could be used for more than just historical analyses. PredPol uses an ML algorithm to calculate where and when crimes could potentially occur. Historical event data sets are used to train the algorithm for each new city (ideally two to five years' worth of data). PredPol then updates the algorithm each day with new events as they are received from the Los Angeles Police Department. After further refinement researchers concluded that crime type, crime location, and crime time/date provide the most accurate input data for forecasting. Results are displayed on so-called PredPol boxes which show the highest-risk areas for each day and the corresponding time frame (Figure 3.2). This helps police officers to anticipate future crimes with the aim of preventing them in the first place. The officers using PredPol are specifically instructed to use 10 percent of their time on patrolling the PredPol boxes.

Operation LASER

Next to PredPol, the Los Angeles Police Department is also interested in predicting who the future offenders will be based on past crime and arrest data. One

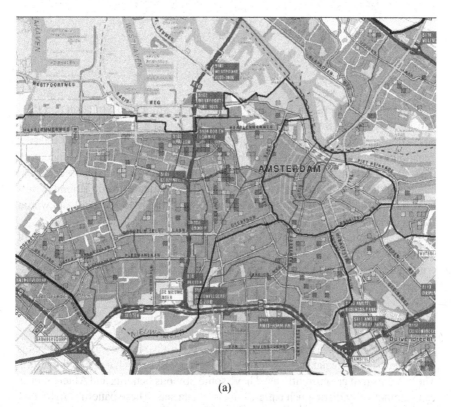

(a)

Figure 3.2 Example output as predicted by CAS[5] on the top and PredPol[6] on the bottom

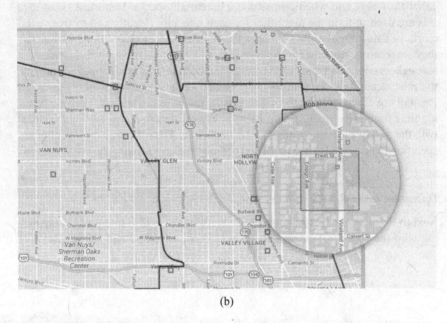

(b)

Figure 3.2 (Continued)

effort, known as Operation LASER[7] (Los Angeles' Strategic Extraction and Restoration; Uchida & Swatt, 2013), which began in 2011, uses information about past offenders over a two-year period, using technology developed by Palantir Technologies, and scores individuals based on their 'rap sheets'. Every encounter with law enforcement is appointed a number of points. The persons scoring the highest in this system are likely to end up on the so-called Chronic Offender Bulletin. This bulletin is a list of people expected to be likely to reoffend and whom should be kept on close watch.

These systems claim to be able to make predictions about where crime will occur, when it is most likely to occur, or even who will commit these future crimes. Critically, these systems come with some pros and cons that will be discussed in the next section.

What are the pros and cons?

It does sound attractive that based on everything we have learned in the past that is documented in large data sets we can predict what will likely happen in the future. The systems that are currently used have some obvious benefits and AI techniques can automatically distinguish patterns in large data sets. These patterns might indicate that certain locations are more prone to criminal activities than other locations. Or, the data might show that criminal activities have a clear spatio-temporal pattern meaning that *certain* criminal activities might happen at *certain* locations within *certain* time frames. One can imagine that pickpocketing is more lucrative during rush hour at a railway station than in the middle of the night in a forest. Systems that are interested in predicting spatio-temporal dynamics (i.e., 'where' and 'when') can be very beneficial for law enforcement. Police officers have a limited amount of time and resources, so a system that allows them to work in a more focused manner would seem to be desirable.

However, systems that tend to predict who is more likely to commit crimes in the future are more prone to critique. When the police focus their attention on a location where no crime activity occurs no one really gets hurt. But what if the police use a system that predicts that someone is more likely to engage in criminal activity than someone else and the system is wrong? This would have quite serious consequences. If the data sets we base our assessments on are not objectively collected or if there are pre existing flaws in the data sets, then the system will learn based on faulty information and come up with an algorithm that is possibly biased. If the police mainly focus their attention on a specific minority group (e.g., based on race) in the first place, that group will be overrepresented in the data set. The focus of the police will then determine that the algorithm will indicate race as very important while making assumptions on future crime predictions. However, that does not mean it represents reality, and the minority group may not in fact be more criminally active than other groups.

COMPAS[8] (Correctional Offender Management Profiling for Alternative Sanctions), developed by Northpointe Inc., is an example of a machine-learning model that has been critiqued for producing biased predictions.[9] It is a risk-assessment algorithm used to predict hot spots of violent crimes, determine the types of supervision inmates might need, and provide information that might be useful in sentencing. COMPAS is also referred to as a black box algorithm, meaning that the developers do not reveal the details of their algorithm. In effect, it is impossible to reliably assess the COMPAS system when the details of the algorithm are unknown (Skeem & Louden, 2007). In short, when the developers chose to keep the details of the algorithm to themselves, the key question becomes: how can outsiders trust the system? They developed a system that may have a big impact on the life course of people, but they refuse to divulge any insight into their methods of prediction. Making predictions of future crimes is already a delicate topic, but if the decision-making algorithm is based on a black box it will likely trigger even more discussion. An investigation by ProPublica[10] found evidence that the COMPAS model might be biased against minorities, but this cannot be confirmed or rejected until full details of the algorithm become public.

TrapWire

Another methodology concerned with detecting threats and prevention of terrorist and criminal events is known as TrapWire.[11] In the aftermath of the attacks of September 11th in the United States, a key government priority was to develop a method that would prevent such (terrorist) attacks from happening in the future. The

TrapWire software uses algorithms and data from a number of surveillance sources to predict potentially criminal/terrorist behaviour. TrapWire recently gained negative attention through the WikiLeaks files that claimed that the software applied a methodology based on a much more widespread and extensive breech of privacy than people were aware of.[12,13] This illustrates another potentially negative aspect of the use of big data in crime prevention: what about privacy?

In order to build a ML model, extremely large data sets need to be collected. This means that many things you do might be monitored, for example, where you go, what you buy, and who you are in contact with, to name only very few. All this data is in turn gathered because there might be an evident association with criminal activity, but in many cases, there probably is no connection whatsoever. Nevertheless, all of the data are required in order to reach these conclusions. But are we willing to hand in a large part of our privacy for a black box method that might incriminate ourselves? To what extent is that even feasible?

What does the future hold for AI within the field of criminology?

AI can be applied in many different ways to benefit the field of crime research and prevention. As discussed earlier, AI makes it possible to discover patterns that were not possible to find by using more traditional research methods. The downside to the use of the large data sets is that to establish such an extensive set of data, one inevitably has to give up some, or possibly much, of his/her privacy.

The potential of AI techniques is currently a prominent discussion outside the field of criminology as well, more specifically in the field of AI itself. In Europe prominent researchers have joined forces in the CLAIRE[14] initiative, in an attempt to establish a European centre of excellence with an emphasis on *human*-centred AI. Similarly, top scientists in the Netherlands have recently launched an AI manifesto[15] regarding the future of AI and the challenges AI faces. In this statement the authors point out the limitations of techniques like ML as well. According to the authors of that manifesto 'AI models simply do not understand the world yet at a level that humans do, and this lack of context makes it very hard for them to generalise to new situations at the same level as humans do'. Humans can learn quickly; they sometimes only need one example, while an ML algorithm needs a large data set of examples to draw on. Humans can interpret the data based on situational circumstances while ML cannot; ML algorithms lack background knowledge and do not have the level of understanding of cause and effect as humans do. So, for example, when an algorithm has been developed to predict crime in Amsterdam, that algorithm cannot directly be used for a different city. The algorithm is tailored to a certain area based on the available data set (e.g., see Chapter 5, this volume). If you want to predict crime in London you will need a new data set to train the algorithm to do so.

Another focus area within the future of AI is called explainable AI, making people understand how algorithms come to their decisions. As AI systems such as ML and decision-making algorithms will significantly affect their users, it is important to be able to explain how and why an AI system produced the effect that it did. The example of COMPAS is a nice illustration of the complications of complex algorithms. Decisions are made but it is unclear what they are precisely based on. The aim in AI is to design tools to help make the systems more transparent. People should be able to understand how advanced AI systems work before they can be used to perform sophisticated tasks.

A third challenge can be described as responsible AI: AI that complies with our norms and standards. Today's complex AI systems have become less predictable while at the same time their potential impact on our society has increased. Hence to guarantee trust in these systems we need to develop algorithms that respect human values. For instance, ML algorithms might adopt the same biases as humans (e.g., with respect to race and gender). When these patterns exist in the data set, the consequences might be critical. Many examples of biased AI systems exist.[16] One of these was discussed earlier in this chapter; when a minority is overrepresented in a police data set because they were racially profiled, the output of the algorithm will be that that minority has a higher probability of committing crimes in the future, when there is in fact the possibility that they actually may be the victim of a biased police corps. Examples of systems based on a biased data set outside the field of criminology exist as well. For example, a recruiting tool for technical jobs used by Amazon that favoured men,[17] or even Google Translate, which translated the gender neutral word 'doctor' from Turkish to a male form in English, while the gender neutral word 'nurse' was supposed to be female.[18]

With the field of AI identifying these key issues as extremely important for future research, we should also take into account that current applications often lack these properties. To develop systems that add to criminological research, it is important that these limitations are acknowledged and solved. You do not want to put someone in prison based on a biased, non-transparent algorithm. One option is to only use data sets that are not biased, to exclude the possibility of unfair predictions. However, since it is not always possible to know whether or not a data set is fair or might be biased, it is very important to realise and accept that there might be some problems and then be very careful about drawing conclusions based on these data sets. As mentioned earlier, it might not be that bad to predict crime at a certain *location* which turns out to be incorrect. But making predictions about *individuals* committing future crimes and attaching consequences should not be allowed when you are not sure about the fairness of the data these predictions are based on. Developing a mechanism that is be able to understand what would be fair, in a way that humans do, is considered to be the holy grail in AI. Extending algorithms with built-in 'fairness' would solve the problem but remains a monumental challenge for now.

To conclude, the possibilities of using AI and especially big data within criminological research are endless but it is up to us to guide this in the right directions, to obtain context-aware, transparent, and unbiased systems that make the world a safer place. It is therefore essential that the research community in computer science puts these societal aspects of AI high on its agenda.

Notes

1 www.scoop.it/u/dahl-winters
2 https://nl.wikipedia.org/wiki/Criminaliteits_Anticipatie_Systeem
3 https://nl.wikipedia.org/wiki/Criminaliteits_Anticipatie_Systeem
4 www.predpol.com/
5 https://nl.wikipedia.org/wiki/Criminaliteits_Anticipatie_Systeem
6 www.predpol.com/
7 Issie Lapowsky. "How the LAPD Uses Data to Predict Crime". www.wired.com/story/los-angeles-police-department-predictive-policing/
8 www.cdcr.ca.gov/rehabilitation/docs/FS_COMPAS_Final_4-15-09.pdf
9 Ed Yong. "A Popular Algorithm Is No Better at Predicting Crimes Than Random People". www.theatlantic.com/technology/archive/2018/01/equivant-compas-algorithm/550646/
10 Julia Angwin, Jeff Larson, Surya Mattu and Lauren Kirchner. "Machine Bias". www.propublica.org/article/machine-bias-risk-assessments-in-criminal-sentencing
11 www.trapwire.com/
12 Charles Arthur. "Trapwire Surveillance System Exposed in Document Leak". www.theguardian.com/world/2012/aug/13/trapwire-surveillance-system-exposed-leak
13 Scott Shane. "WikiLeaks Stirs Global Fears on Antiterrorist Software". www.nytimes.com/2012/08/14/us/trapwire-antiterrorist-software-leaks-set-off-web-furor.html
14 https://claire-ai.org/
15 Special Interest Group on Artificial Intelligence. http://ii.tudelft.nl/bnvki/wp-content/uploads/2018/09/Dutch-AI-Manifesto.pdf
16 Daniel Cossins. "Discriminating Algorithms: 5 Times AI Showed Prejudice". www.newscientist.com/article/2166207-discriminating-algorithms-5-times-ai-showed-prejudice/
17 "Amazon Ditched AI Recruiting Tool that Favored Men for Technical Jobs". www.theguardian.com/technology/2018/oct/10/amazon-hiring-ai-gender-bias-recruiting-engine
18 Adam Hadhazy. "Biased Bots: Artificial-Intelligence Systems Echo Human Prejudices". www.princeton.edu/news/2017/04/18/biased-bots-artificial-intelligence-systems-echo-human-prejudices

References

Bhattacharyya, S., Jha, S., Tharakunnel, K., & Westland, J. C. (2011). Data mining for credit card fraud: A comparative study. *Decision Support Systems*, *50*(3), 602–613, Elsevier.

Bishop, C. M. (2006). *Pattern recognition and machine learning*. New York, NY: Springer.

Chen, H., Chung, W., Qin, Y., Chau, M., Xu, J. J., Wang, G., . . . Atabakhsh, H. (2003). Crime data mining: An overview and case studies. *National Conference on Digital Government Research*, 1–5. Boston, MA.

Chen, H., Chung, W., Xu, J. J., Wang, G., Qin, Y., & Chau, M. (2004). Crime data mining: A general framework and some examples. *Computer*, *37*(4), 50–56.

Chiranjeevi, C. B., & Revathy, R. (2015). Drug trafficking suspect prediction using data mining. *International Journal of Advanced Research in Computer Science and Software Engineering*, *5*(8).

Dick, P. K. (1956). The minority report. *Short Story in Fantastic Universe*, *4*(6).

Friedman, J. H. (1998). Data mining and statistics: What's the connection? *Computing Science and Statistics*, *29*(1), 3–9.

Gerber, M. (2014). Predicting crime using Twitter and kernel density estimation. *Decision Support Systems*, *61*, 115–125.

Gerritsen, C., & Van Breda, W. (2015). Simulation-based prediction of collective emotional states. Proceedings of the *International Conference on Social Computing and Social Media*, LNCS, 118–126, Springer.

Kohavi, R., & Provost, F. (1998). Glossary of terms. *Machine Learning, 30,* 271–274.

Lin, Y., Chen, T., & Yu, L. (2017). Using machine learning to assist crime prevention. Proceedings of the *6th IIAI International Congress on Advanced Applied Informatics (IIAI-AAI),* 1029–1030. Hamamatsu, Japan.

McClendon, L., & Meghanathan, N. (2015). Using machine learning algorithms to analyze crime data. *Machine Learning and Applications: An International Journal (MLAIJ), 2*(1). doi:10.5121/mlaij.2015.2101.1

Pang, B., & Lee, L. (2008). Opinion mining and sentiment analysis. *Foundations and Trends in Information Retrieval, 2*(1–2), 1–135.

Perry, W. L., & McInnis, B. (2013). *Predictive policing: The role of crime forecasting in law enforcement operations.* Santa Monica, CA: RAND.

Rienks, R. (2015). *Predictive policing: Taking a chance for a safer future.* Korpsmedia, PDC.

Samuel, A. (1959). Some studies in machine learning using the game of checkers. *Journal of Research and Development, 3*(3), 210–229, IDM.

Siegel, E. (2013). *Predictive analytics: The power to predict who will click, buy, lie or die.* Hoboken, NJ: John Wiley and Sons Inc.

Skeem, J. L., & Louden, J. E. (2007). *Assessment of evidence on the quality of the Correctional Offender Management Profiling for Alternative Sanctions (COMPAS).* file:///C:/Users/Elgenaar/Downloads/Assessment_of_Evidence_on_the_Quality_of_the_Corre%20(1).pdf

Uchida, C. D., & Swatt, M. L. (2013). Operation LASER and the effectiveness of hot spot patrol: A panel analysis. *Police Quarterly, 16*(3), 287–304, Sage.

4 Future applications of big data in environmental criminology

Mohammad Tayebi, Uwe Glässer, and Martin A. Andresen

Introduction

Big data are increasingly becoming a topic in research in both the physical and the social sciences. Though its definition has been a moving target with increasingly powerful computers, big data is generally defined as extremely large or complex (i.e., multiple dimensions) data sets that need to be analysed using methods outside of the traditional data-processing applications commonly used. These data have significantly increased the possibilities for analysis of new topics but also presenting new opportunities to re-visit only questions in new ways.

Big data are increasingly being used in criminology and, specifically, environmental criminology. Environmental criminology is primarily concerned with the analysis of crime through a spatial and temporal lens. Topics can range from crime prevention to policing to theoretical testing, but spatial and temporal methods are at the heart of much of this research. These added dimensions of space and time alone could turn 'small data' into big data, but there is also a trend of environmental criminology using smaller and smaller units of analysis that leads to a greater number of observations in the data sets environmental criminologists use (Weisburd, Bruinsma, & Bernasco, 2009).

In this chapter we discuss some of the potential uses of big data and its associated computational methods for the future of environmental criminology. There are aspects of research in which big data has already been used. We discuss some of this research, but also new directions. We conclude with a brief discussion of the considerations that must be taken into account with the use of this new data source in future research.

Making better small data with big data

Though big data is often used an analysed as a whole, we would also argue that pieces of big data can be used to make the small data we use in criminology better. For example, some research within environmental criminology has used satellite data, social media data, and mobile phone data to measure where people are in order to better identify risky places (Andresen, 2011; Malleson & Andresen, 2015a, 2015b, 2016). Because such data may better represent where people are through the geo-referencing of social media and mobile phone networks, they can be useful in identifying where people are, on average (rather than census data), or where they are on particular days of the week, or times within a given day. Given that there are hundreds of millions of tweets every day alone, specialised statistical and computing techniques are necessary to be able to analyse these data. However, most often, researchers in environmental criminology are interested in particular places. These places could be the size of cities, but also the size of a street segment (Andresen et al., 2017a, 2017b; Hodgkinson, Andresen, & Farrell, 2016).

Within these contexts of cartographically larger places, social media or mobile phone information can be obtained to better identify where people are and when they are there. This leads to the better identification of risk for different places and those places at different times of the day. This is what has been done, but the potential for such analyses has only begun to be utilised. There are a number of confidentiality and ethical implications for these types of analyses (to be discussed further later), but the potential for understanding crime patterns (spatially and temporally, among others) is tremendous with the availability of big data.

For example, knowing the age and gender of people, how long they spend at particular places, and their spending habits can all be instructive for understanding why offending and victimisation occurs here and there, now and not then. These data can be identified from larger big data data sets for smaller areas and then aggregated to protect confidentiality. Such data could then be used in traditional (statistical) analyses to better measure theoretical constructs, testing theory in ways would simply could not do before. But the presence and availability of big data should not only be used to revisit old methods in new ways but open the door for new types of analyses and pushing the field of environmental criminology forward.

Big data, data mining, and machine learning in environmental criminology

One of the ways in which environmental criminology may move forward with big data is through the use of modern computing techniques such as data mining and machine learning. Generally speaking, data mining involves the identification of patterns in big data that are not feasible, or extremely costly in terms of time and/or money; machine learning is one method within data mining that uses algorithms and statistical modelling without explicit instructions. In other words, these techniques rely less on theory guiding what we think should be in the model than on inference itself. As such, all the data available can be used to test theoretical models and policy implementation, rather than a relatively small set of data our theories tell us should matter.

For example, studies that use census data for predictor variables rarely use more than 10 to 20 predictor variables when there are hundreds of such variables available through most censuses. Data mining can be used for inferential testing of all these variables and their interactions that is simply not tractable using conventional techniques. Moreover, with the availability of crime and police data at relatively fine spatial resolutions for many police agencies across many countries (sometimes available over many years), data mining techniques can be used to analyse crime patterns at multiple scales (spatially and temporally), across multiple crime types, across multiple policing services, using predictors that have not been able to be incorporated before because of data, software, and user limitations. The implications of such data and methods are significant for the testing of our theories across many different contexts with similarly defined data and the evaluation of larger scale policies that may work in some places but not others.

Another potential with the use of big data and data mining is the testing of theories that have simply not been possible in the past. For example, the theoretical construct of the geometry of crime requires activity patterns for offenders and non-offenders, alike to be able to test the predictions of this theory. These activity patterns need to be for both deviant and non-deviant activities and measured over time in order to know where and when people travel to their activity nodes and the pathways between them. These data could be identified through mobile phone activity, for example, and then cross checked with victimisation and offending data. Hypotheses and propositions that have never been fully tested in the past can be tested using big data and its corresponding methods.

Predictive analysis and big data

Turning to more predictive analyses that are already being undertaken but need further development, policymakers inevitably face enormous challenges deploying notoriously scarce resources ever more efficiently to apprehend criminals, disrupt criminal networks, and effectively deter crime by investing in crime reduction and prevention strategies. While data collection from different sources, data preparation and information sharing pose difficult tasks, the big challenge for law enforcement agencies is analysing and extracting knowledge from their large collection of crime data. Applying data-driven approaches on such data can provide a scientific foundation for developing effective crime reduction and prevention strategies through analysis of offenders' spatial decision making and their social standing. The main idea behind crime prediction techniques is that crime is not random but happens in a patterned manner. In the crime data mining process, the goal is to understand criminal behaviours and extract criminal patterns in order to predict crime and take steps to prevent it.

The rapid evolution of data science, employing techniques and theories drawn from broad areas such as machine learning and data mining, through availability of massive computational power increasingly influences our daily lives. Data are collected, modelled, and analysed to uncover the patterns of human behaviour and help with predicting social trends. This is changing the way we think about business, politics, education, health, and data science innovations will undoubtedly continue in the years to come. One particular area that has seen limited growth in accepting and using these powerful tools is public safety. This is somewhat surprising given the important role that predictive analytics can play in public safety.

New methodologies emerging in data science can advance crime analysis to the next level through the use of big data and move from tracking patterns of crime to predicting those patterns. This has led to a new paradigm of crime analysis, called predictive policing. Predictive policing uses data science and big data to identify potential targets for criminal activity with the goal of crime prevention. Successful predictive policing results in more proactive policing and less reactive policing.

Specifically, 'predictive policing refers to any policing strategy or tactic that develops and uses information and advanced analysis to inform forward-thinking crime prevention' (Uchida, 2012), which involves multiple disciplines to form the rules and develop the models. Given that research strongly supports that crime is not random but rather occurs in patterns, the goal of predictive policing methods is to extract crime patterns from historical data at both macro and micro scales as a basis for prediction and prevention of future crimes. This approach uses data-driven tools and big data that benefit from data mining and machine learning techniques for predicting crime locations and temporal characteristics of criminal behaviour.

Predictive analysis for policing can be divided into four classes:

- **Predicting offenders**. The goal is predicting future offenders using the history of individuals such as features of their living environment and behavioural patterns.
- **Predicting victims**. This is about identifying individuals who more likely than others may become victims and predicting risky situations for potential victims.
- **Predicting crime locations**. This task aims at predicting the location of future crimes at individual and aggregate level. An important aspect of crime is the geographic location that crime happens. Every neighbourhood provides some condition in which criminal behaviour takes place, but crime distribution in city neighbourhoods is not even. Understanding the spatial patterns of crime is essential for law enforcement agencies to design efficient crime reduction and prevention policies. Although mining spatial patterns of crime data in the aggregate level took special attention in the criminology literature, there is not that much work about crime spatial patterns for individual offenders.
- **Predicting criminal collaborations**. This involves predicting likely future collaboration between offenders and the type of associated crime using social network analysis. We focus our discussion on this latter topic area.

Co-offending network analysis

Social networks represent relationships among social entities. Normally, such relationships can be represented as a network. Examples include interactions between members of a group (such as family, friends, or neighbours) or economic relationships between businesses. Social networks are important in many respects. Social influence may motivate someone to buy a product, to commit a crime, and any other decision can be interpreted and modelled under a social network structure. Spread of diseases such as AIDS infection, the diffusion of information, and word of mouth also strongly depend on the topology of social networks.

Social network analysis (SNA) focuses on structural aspects of networks to detect and interpret the patterns of social entities. SNA essentially takes a network with nodes and edges and finds distinguished properties of the network through formal analysis. Data mining is the process of finding patterns and knowledge hidden in large databases. Data mining methods are increasingly being applied to social networks, and there is substantial overlap and synergy with SNA. These methods are particularly important for the combinations and permutations of possible social ties or links when using large data sets (big data). For example, even a criminal event data set with only a few thousand criminal events leads to crime linkage pairs in the millions that are difficult to analyse when considering traditional data analyses.

New techniques for the analysis and mining of social networks are developed for a broad range of domains, including health and criminology. These methods can be categorised depending on the level of granularity at which the network is analysed: 1) methods that determine properties of the social network as a whole; 2) methods that discover important subnetworks; 3) methods that analyse individual network nodes; and 4) methods that characterise network evolution. In the following, we list the primary tasks of SNA:

- **Centrality analysis** aims at determining more important actors of a social network so as to understand their prestige, importance, or influence in a network;
- **Community detection** methods identify groups of actors that are more densely connected among each other than with the rest of the network;
- **Information diffusion** studies the flow of information through networks and proposes abstract models of that diffusion such as the Independent Cascade model;
- **Link prediction** aims at predicting for a given social network how its structure evolves over time, that is, which new links are likely to form; and
- **Generative models** are probabilistic models that simulate the topology, temporal dynamics, and patterns of large real-world networks.

Co-offending networks

Criminal organisational systems differ in terms of their scope, form, and content. They can be a simple co-offending looking for opportunistic crimes, or a complex organised crime group involved in serious crimes. They can be formed based on one-time partnership for committing a crime, or their existence can have continuity over time and across different crime types. For example, in a criminal organisation system interaction among actors can be initiated from family, friendship, ethnic or other possible ties.

A co-offending network is a network of offenders who have committed crimes together. With increasing attention to SNA, law enforcement and intelligence agencies have come to realise the importance of detailed knowledge about co-offending networks. Groups and organisations that engage in conspiracies, terrorist activities, and crimes such as drug trafficking typically do this in a concealed fashion, trying to hide their illegal activities. In analysing such activities, investigations do not only focus on individual suspects but also examine criminal groups and illegal organisation and their behaviour.

Thus, it is important to identify co-offending networks in data resources readily available to investigators, such as police arrest data and court data, and study them using social network analysis methods. In turn, social network analysis can provide useful information about individuals as well. For example, investigators could determine who are key players, and subject them to closer inspection. In general, knowledge about co-offending network structures provides a basis for law enforcement agencies to make strategic or tactical decisions.

Co-offending network analysis in practice

Co-offending networks analysis contributes to predictive policing by detecting hidden links and predicting potential links among offenders. In this section, we introduce important applications of co-offending networks analysis in predictive policing that are covered in this research.

Organised crime group detection

Organised crime is a major international concern. Organised crime groups produce disproportionate harm to societies, and an increasing volume of violence is related to their activities. Because the primary aim of organised crime groups is gaining material benefit, they try to access to resources that can be profitably exploited. In terms of economic-related crimes (e.g., credit and debit card fraud), organised crime costs tax payers billions of dollars per year.

Understanding the structure of organised crime groups and the factors that impact on it is crucial to combat organised crime. There are several possible perspectives how to define the structure of organised crime groups, but recent criminological studies are increasingly focusing on using social network analysis for this purpose. The idea of using social network analysis is that links between offenders and subgroups of an organised crime group are critical determinant of the performance and sustainability of organised crime groups.

Confronted with a bewildering diversity of characteristics referred to in existing definitions of organised crime and criminal organisations, the conceptual model itself appears not clearly rendered in the literature. Striving for a definition that is general and open, a potential source is the criminal code, although this depends on a specific country. For instance, a baseline definition of criminal organisation is provided by the Criminal Code of Canada:

In Canada a criminal organization is a group, however organized that: (a) is composed of three or more persons in or outside Canada; and (b) has as one of its main purposes or main activities the facilitation or commission of one or more serious offences, that, if committed, would likely result in the direct or indirect receipt of a material benefit, including a financial benefit, by the group or by any one of the persons who constitute the group. The definition further specifies that it excludes a group of three or more persons that has formed randomly for the immediate commission of a single offence.

(Section 467.1(1) of the Criminal Code of Canada)

Looking for a quantitative definition, in an attempt to measure organised crime, van der Heijden (1996) proposes a number of common characteristics:

1 Collaboration of more than two people;
2 Commission of serious criminal offences (suspected);
3 Determined by the pursuit of profit and/or power;
4 Each having their own appointed tasks;
5 For a prolonged or indefinite period of time;
6 Using some form of discipline and control;
7 Operating across borders;
8 Using violence or other means suitable for intimidation;
9 Using commercial or business-like structures;
10 Engaged in money laundering;
11 Exerting influence on politics, the media, public administration, judicial authorities, or economy.

According to van der Heijden (1996), for any criminal group to be categorised as organised crime it needs to have at least six of these characteristics, where items 1, 2, and 3 are obligatory, thus adding three more characteristics. A major study in the Netherlands (Fijnaut, 1998, p. 27) mentions great variations in collaborative forms of organised crime and concludes that

the frameworks need not necessarily exhibit the hierarchical structure or meticulous division of labor often attributed to mafia syndicates. Intersections of social networks with a rudimentary division of labor have also been included as groups in the sub-report on the role of Dutch criminal groups, where they are referred to as cliques.

An impressive collection of definitions of organised crime specific for various countries, comprising more than individual 150 entries in total, has been gathered by von Lampe (2019). In addition, this collection also includes comments on how to define organised crime, and definitions by prominent individuals and government agencies, for instance, such as the Federal Bureau of Investigation (FBI). Not included though are definitions of the term 'organised crime group'. Given the abstract nature and informal language of these definitions, it is not clear at all how and to what extent one may utilise this resource for defining organised crime in precise computational and/or mathematical terms. The use of big data and its corresponding analytic techniques come into play here because various forms of law enforcement data can be used to show how offenders interact from the ground up and identify potentially organised behaviour (using all of the available data), rather than imposing a definition *a priori* and then searching for interactions that are consistent with that definition.

Organised crime group detection using community detection

In most cases, existing definitions in the literature on organised crime concentrate on three essential perspectives for characterising the nature of this form of crime (von Lampe, 2019). First, organised crime is primarily about crime, such that organised crime is seen as a specific type of criminal activity that has certain specific characteristics (continuity, in contrast to irregular criminal behaviour). Second, organised crime is related to the concentration of power, either in economic or in political structures of the society. Third, the emphasis is on being organised. That is, the important aspect of organised crime is on how offenders are connected to each other more than what they do.

Based on the third view, we can formalise central aspects of criminal networks in a coherent and consistent formal framework to provide a precise semantic foundation that is consistent with criminological research, social network analysis, and law enforcement operations. Such work would aim at bridging the conceptual gap between data level, mining level and interpretation level, and is intended for developing advanced computational methods for analysing co-offending networks to detect and extract organised crime structures and how they evolve over time in order to assist law enforcement and intelligence agencies in their investigations.

Community detection in social networks has attracted considerable interest and many definitions of the concept of community have been proposed. In social science studies, social networks are considered as basis of social behaviours and activities. Studies of different social networks show that community structure influences information transfer, communication, and cooperation. Sense of community is generally defined as a feeling that members of a group matter to one another and to the group, and a common belief that members' needs will be satisfied through their commitment to be together. The nature of organised crime groups, however, is different from other types of groups such as friendship or co-authorship groups. Organised crime groups are usually well established with group membership being defined explicitly and strictly. Unlike friendship or co-authorship communities, offender groups as well are characterised by member relationships that are more systematic and organised to achieve material benefit from committing crime. Therefore, detecting organised crime groups calls for a stricter definition of community. Given the large volumes of law enforcement data, analysing and extracting knowledge from their data using data-driven approaches such as machine learning, as discussed earlier, can help define what matters for organised crime groups that is different from other forms of groups to better identify their presence.

On this note, and based on fundamental discussions in the criminology literature, one can summarise the important characteristics of organised crime groups
as follows: 1) these groups have at least three members and can be categorised
as centralised or distributed or hierarchical groups, but the focus is on offender
groups for which the density of their intra-group collaborations is higher than
the density of intergroup collaborations; 2) organised crime groups are characterised by a distribution of roles and different degrees of agency among individuals,
where groups can overlap and may have common members; 3) these groups commit serious crimes with the perspective of gaining material benefit; and 4) their
activity is more continuous compared to regular offender groups. Using big data
analytics, these characteristics of organised crime groups can be searched and
then tested with regard to their validity on a grand scale with all possible combinations. Moreover, predictive analytics can then be used to identify the potential
emergence of these characteristics in real time.

Therefore, for the purpose of organised crime group detection, in each time
snapshot of a co-offending network the following tasks are carried out in consecutive steps: 1) discover offender groups in the current network; 2) compute
the activity and criminality of these groups in the time period between the current
network and the previous network based on the offences that were committed by
their members; 3) assess the material benefit associated with each of the offences
considered in Step 2; 4) identify those groups that qualify as possible criminal
organisations; 5) update the groups evolutionary trace for the current time period.
It should be clear at this point that sophisticated data mining techniques become
critical with the increasingly complexity of such analyses. For example, rather than
relying on traditional policing methods to identify organised crime groups, police
calls for service data with co-offender identifiers can be used to identify clusters
of individuals who may then be assigned to these more formal group relationships.
But before such analyses can take place, identifying all co-offences is critical.

Co-offence prediction

Co-offence prediction is defined as a link prediction problem for co-offending
networks. In the context of suspect investigation, law enforcement can more precisely focus their efforts based on probable relationships in criminal networks
that have previously not observed. Traditional suspect investigation methods use
partial knowledge discovered from crime scenes to identify potential suspects.
Co-offending networks analysis provides a complementary approach to traditional criminal profiling methods insofar as it can contribute to investigation in
cases where multiple offenders committed a crime, but only a subset of offenders
are charged. Therefore, link prediction is an important aspect of social network
analysis with the aim to better understand the network structure. Link prediction
methods can be used to extract missing information, identify hidden interactions,
and evaluate network evolution mechanisms. For example, missing one key player
in a criminal network (who may or may not be directly related to each crime in a

law enforcement database) could bring together or solidify an existing network structure.

Contrary to other social networks, the concealment of identities and activities of actors is a central characteristic of co-offending networks. Still, the network topology is a primary source of information for co-offence prediction. Moreover, there are two other major information sources: environmental activity and criminal activity. Offenders who are spatially close tend to be socially close, because this increases the chance of meeting each other and forming new criminal collaborations (Tayebi, Frank, & Glässer, 2012). Further, common criminal experience (with the same type of offences, for example) also affects co-offending behaviour (Weerman, 2003).

Several studies now show that supervised link prediction approaches outperform unsupervised methods (Lichtenwalter, Lussier, & Chawla, 2010) who use only topological features (Liben-Nowell & Kleinberg, 2007). In contrast to unsupervised methods, supervised learning methods can overcome the class imbalance problem, an issue that arises when the ratio of groupings of data (co-offending or not, for example) is not close to one-to-one (Lichtenwalter et al., 2010). Exploiting the geographic information provided by location-based social networks services, some recently proposed link prediction methods consider spatial characteristics of users (Scellato, Noulas, & Mascolo, 2011; Wang, Pedreschi, Song, Giannotti, & Barabasi, 2011). Scellato and colleagues (2011) used information about places visited by users, in addition to their social network features, to define prediction spaces that reduce the class imbalance ratio and improve the prediction of people to people and people to places.

Co-offending networks are spatially embedded in a manner similar to location-based social networks. However, the environmental effects on the formation of co-offence links and, accordingly, our approach in defining offenders' spatial closeness are different from those in location-based social networks (Scellato et al., 2011; Wang et al., 2011; Zhang, Shou, Chen, Chen, & Bei, 2012; Cho, Myers, & Leskovec, 2011). Tayebi, Ester, Glässer, and Brantingham (2014) proposed a framework that builds on criminological theories (Brantingham & Brantingham, 1981; Brantingham, Brantingham, & Andresen, 2017; McGloin, Sullivan, Piquero, & Bacon, 2008; Morselli, 2009; Rossmo, 2000; Sutherland & Cressey, 1947) and, considering the available information on offenders, distinguishes three different criminal cooperation opportunities: socially related, geographically related, and experience-related. In this work, the authors studied the co-offence prediction problem in each of these prediction spaces separately, achieving two goals. First, the heavy class imbalance between positive (existing links) and negative samples (non-existing links) is the main challenge of the link prediction problem (Lichtenwalter et al., 2010). The restriction of the training and test data to the different prediction spaces reduces the class imbalance ratio significantly, while keeping about half of the positive samples (co-offences). Second, the prediction spaces enhance the understanding of co-offence patterns in different criminal cooperation opportunities.

They define the prediction features in four different categories (social, geographic, geo-social, and similarity), and evaluate their prediction strength both individually and as a set. Social features indicate social closeness of offenders based on their position in a co-offending network. Geographic features show spatial proximity of offenders based on their residential locations and the location of offences they have committed. Geo-social features combine social and geographic characteristics of offenders. Finally, similarity features capture homophily-based characteristics of offenders, such as age and gender. Evaluating features individually and also as a set shows that the geo-social features we define outperform other features.

The co-offence prediction framework proposed aims at advancing the state-of-the-art in crime data mining by making the following contributions: 1) defining co-offence prediction spaces to reduce the class imbalance; 2) introducing novel prediction features for co-offence prediction; and 3) experimentally evaluating the proposed approach on large real-world crime data. Some of the main findings in this research include results that show that social and geographic features have important implications for the evaluation of networks. First, repeated exposure to individuals is a strong predictor compared to the social features present with common friends in the network. This implies that the chance of criminal collaboration increases more with the opportunity to commit crimes than with trust or transitivity in the co-offending network. Crime location distance is a better predictor of co-offending than home location distance, meaning that being criminally active in close proximity may lead to new criminal collaboration. Second, geo-social features are better co-offence predictors than geographic or social features alone. This result implies that researchers and practitioners need to focus more on combined patterns in environmental and social features to enhance crime reduction and prevention. This also shows the role of environmental criminology in the context of co-offending. Third, experimental results show that, although there is variability in the performance of different classifiers (e.g., the area under the receiver operating characteristic (ROC) curves), the probability of predicting a co-offence for similarity-related offenders is higher than for socially or geographically related co-offenders.

Taken together, this information can then be used in the context of co-offending network disruption. Actors of a social network can be categorised based on their relations in the network. Actors in the same category may take similar roles within an organisation, community, or whole network. These roles are usually dependent on the network structure and the actors' position in the network. For instance, actors who are located in the central positions of a social network may be detected as key players in that network. Actors who are connected to many other actors may be viewed as socially active players, and actors who are frequently observed by other actors may be identified as popular players.

In terms of co-offending network disruption, the goal is finding a set of players whose removal creates a network with the least possible cohesion. In the other words, their removal maximally destabilises the network. This task is critical in the co-offending network analysis where removing the key players may sabotage the network and decrease the aggregate crime rate. Given the large volume of law enforcement data, big data and its corresponding analytic techniques can be used to identify these players, at times using co-offence prediction techniques, and then simulating the impact of their removal to better understand where scarce law enforcement resources may be best allocated.

Directions and issues moving forward for big data in environmental criminology

As stated previously, thousands of criminal events can have millions of crime pairs, so tens of thousands of criminal events (not a large data set in the grand scheme of things) can have hundreds of millions of crime pairs. As such, what may be traditionally considered 'small data' becomes big data through the addition of inherent complexity within the small data (new dimensions are created and added), requiring the application of data mining techniques to make the analysis tractable. Therefore, it is important to note that the use of big data, or the transformation of small data to big data, has implications for social science (e.g., environmental criminology) research. There are two primary considerations in the future of big data in environmental criminology: 1) the need for specialised knowledge and 2) ethics in the use of big data. Each is discussed in turn.

The need for specialised knowledge is not a limitation or cautionary aspect of big data, but a pragmatic concern. Though there are social scientists (environmental criminologists) with the necessary computing skills to undertake the computational methods necessary for the analysis of big data, most often it will be necessary for environmental criminologists to collaborate with other scholars from fields such as computing science and statistics. At face value, this is a simple task, but it is important to recognise that different disciplines have different research and publication cultures. Some differences involve where research is published, author order, and the number of authors, among many others. These aforementioned differences, for example, need to be known up front and accounted for when publications are 'counted' for salary and promotion decisions. One of the most pertinent publication cultural differences between the social sciences and computing science is publishing in traditional journals and conference proceedings. In the social sciences, conferences proceedings are viewed as a lesser publication form, deemed to not have the same rigour and value as an article in a peer-reviewed journal. However, conference proceedings in computing science undergo similar levels of peer-review as traditional journals in the social sciences in terms of the peer-review process and rejection rates. It can be difficult to assess academic outlets across disciplines, but if interdisciplinary research is to move forward, cultural differences such as these, along with many others, must be figured out and accounted for to ensure fairness in measuring academic output that is truly interdisciplinary.

With regard to ethics and big data, privacy concerns increase in magnitude almost as quickly as the sizes of 'big data' data sets themselves. Environmental criminologists, in particular, analyse sensitive data sets with regard to criminal behaviour or victimisation. Even without personal identifiers, the same methods used to analyse big data can be used to create data-linkages across different data sets, placing personal identification at risk. For example, with the large volumes of social media data that may have information regarding when and where someone was as well as what they were doing (or what happened to them), criminal offending or victimisation may be able to be connected to specific individuals. With larger and more data sets, this probabilistic matching becomes more of a concern. This is only one example but shows the importance of asking new questions of not just if we can do something, but if we even should.

Despite these considerations for the need of specialised knowledge and the ethical concerns, the potential for the continued and advanced use of big data in environmental criminology is great. What has been done has made significant advances in the field and what will be done in the future is expected to alter the ways in which we think about environmental criminology as a discipline.

References

Andresen, M. A. (2011). The ambient population and crime analysis. *Professional Geographer*, *63*(2), 193–212.

Andresen, M. A., Curman, A. S. N., & Linning, S. J. (2017a). The trajectories of crime at places: Understanding the patterns of disaggregated crime types. *Journal of Quantitative Criminology*, *33*(3), 427–449.

Andresen, M. A., Linning, S. J., & Malleson, N. (2017b). Crime at places and spatial concentrations: Exploring the spatial stability of property crime in Vancouver BC, 2003–2013. *Journal of Quantitative Criminology*, *33*(2), 255–275.

Brantingham, P. J., & Brantingham, P. L. (Eds.). (1981). *Environmental criminology*. Beverly Hills, CA: Sage Publications.

Brantingham, P. J., Brantingham, P. L., & Andresen, M. A. (2017). The geometry of crime and crime pattern theory. In R. Wortley & M. Townsley (Eds.), *Environmental criminology and crime analysis* (2nd ed., pp. 98–115). New York, NY: Routledge.

Cho, E., Myers, S. A., & Leskovec, J. (2011). Friendship and mobility: User movement in location-based social networks. Proceedings of the *17th ACM SIGKDD International Conference on Knowledge Discovery and Data Mining*, 1082–1090. San Diego, CA.

Fijnaut, C., Bovenkerk, F., Bruinsma, G., & van de Bunt, H. (1998). *Organized crime in the Netherlands*. The Hague, Netherlands: Kluwer Law International.

Hodgkinson, T., Andresen, M. A., & Farrell, G. (2016). The decline and locational shift of automotive theft: A local level analysis. *Journal of Criminal Justice*, *44*(1), 49–57.

Liben-Nowell, D., & Kleinberg, J. (2007). The link-prediction problem for social networks. *Journal of the Association for Information Science and Technology*, *58*(7), 1019–1031.

Lichtenwalter, R. N., Lussier, J. T., & Chawla, N. V. (2010). New perspectives and methods in link prediction. Proceedings of the *16th ACM SIGKDD International Conference on Knowledge Discovery and Data Mining*, 243–252. Washington, DC.

Malleson, N., & Andresen, M. A. (2015a). Spatio-temporal crime hotspots and the ambient population. *Crime Science*, *4*(10).

Malleson, N., & Andresen, M. A. (2015b). The impact of using social media data in crime rate calculations: Shifting hot spots and changing spatial patterns. *Cartography and Geographic Information Science*, *42*(2), 112–121.

Malleson, N., & Andresen, M. A. (2016). Exploring the impact of ambient population measures on London crime hotspots. *Journal of Criminal Justice, 46,* 52–63.

McGloin, J. M., Sullivan, C. J., Piquero, A. R., & Bacon, S. (2008). Investigating the stability of co-offending and co-offenders among a sample of youthful offenders. *Criminology, 46*(1), 155–188.

Morselli, C. (2009). *Inside criminal networks.* New York, NY: Springer.

Rossmo, D. K. (2000). *Geographic profiling.* Boca Raton, FL: CRC Press.

Scellato, S., Noulas, A., & Mascolo, C. (2011). Exploiting place features in link prediction on location-based social networks. Proceedings of the *17th ACM SIGKDD International Conference on Knowledge Discovery and Data Mining,* 1046–1054. San Diego, CA.

Sutherland, E. H., & Cressey, D. R. (1947). *Principles of criminology* (4th ed.). Chicago, IL: J.B. Lippincott.

Tayebi, M. A., Ester, M., Glässer, U., & Brantingham, P. L. (2014). Spatially embedded co-offence prediction using supervised learning. Proceedings of the *20th ACM SIGKDD International Conference on Knowledge Discovery and Data Mining,* 1789–1798. New York, NY.

Tayebi, M. A., Frank, R., & Glässer, U. (2012). Understanding the link between social and spatial distance in the crime world. Proceedings of the *20th ACM SIGSPATIAL International Conference on Advances in Geographic Information Systems,* 550–553. New York, NY.

Uchida, C. (2012). *A national discussion on predictive policing: Defining our terms and mapping successful implementation strategies.* Washington, DC: National Institute of Justice.

van der Heijden, T. (1996). Measuring organized crime in Western Europe. In *Policing in Central and Eastern Europe: Comparing first hand knowledge with experience from the West.* Slovenia: College of Police and Security Studies.

von Lampe, K. (2019, February 8). *Definitions of organized crime.* Retrieved from www.organized-crime.de/organizedcrimedefinitions.htm.

Wang, D., Pedreschi, D., Song, C., Giannotti, F., & Barabasi, A.-L. (2011). Human mobility, social ties, and link prediction. Proceedings of the *17th ACM SIGKDD International Conference on Knowledge Discovery and Data Mining,* 1100–1108. San Diego, CA.

Weerman, F. M. (2003). Co-offending as social exchange: Explaining characteristics of co-offending. *British Journal of Criminology, 43*(2), 398–416.

Weisburd, D., Bruinsma, G. J. N., & Bernasco, W. (2009). Units of analysis in geographic criminology: Historical development, critical issues, and open questions. In D. Weisburd, W. Bernasco, & G. J. N. Bruinsma (Eds.), *Putting crime in its place: Units of analysis in geographic criminology* (pp. 3–31). New York, NY: Springer.

Zhang, C., Shou, L., Chen, K., Chen, G., & Bei, Y. (2012). Evaluating geo-social influence in location-based social networks. Proceedings of the *21st ACM International Conference on Information and Knowledge Management,* 1442–1451. Maui, HI.

5 Leveraging police incident data for intelligence-led policing

David B. Skillicorn, Christian Leuprecht, and Alexandra Green

Introduction

Police often claim that they, and their investigations, are intelligence led. By and large, this is hyperbole. Operationally, police investigations remain investigator-led: the investigator decides what to investigate and when, then provides direction for what information to collect in support of an investigation. This is especially true of investigations once a crime has occurred where the focus is on the evidentiary value of information, rather than its intelligence value.

Strategically, police tend to have an impoverished understanding of the threat environment as it emerges and evolves because they do not have access to the requisite data, their data are unsystematic and/or incomplete, or they have limited capacity to analyse the data at their disposal to conduct a robust and reliable environmental and horizon scan. The objective of this article is to demonstrate the empirical value of applying advanced methodological techniques to a data set of incident records that virtually all police forces collect and retain: their Records Management System (RMS). However, the findings also lead us to formulate a new theory built on an old idea: co-offenders and the 'social networks' induced from co-offending are well established in the literature (e.g., Papachristos, Braga, Piza, & Grossman, 2015); however, the findings here suggest an analogous theory of co-presence networks – including people who interact regularly with police, who do not necessarily end up being charged (witnesses and victims), but who nonetheless occupy positional advantage within the structure of the RMS incident data network.

We present an exploratory analysis of incident Record Management System data provided by Kingston Police. Kingston is a medium-sized city, with a population of about 125,000 and covering an area of 91 square kilometres, in Eastern Ontario, Canada. Kingston Police incident reports for 2015 were pulled from the RMS database where they are recorded. An incident is any interaction between the general population and police: this includes police attendance at crime scenes, but also civilian interactions at the police station (for example, to report a car accident) or by phone or online. In 2015, there were 46,668 incident records, and 188 attributes potentially associated with each record. Records contain information about the date, time, and place of each incident, the individuals concerned, and specific aspects relevant to each kind of incident. Some attributes are numeric, some are times and dates, some are identifiers, and some are free-form text (addresses, officer comments, data about resolution).

At present, such data are commonly used in two ways. First, they may be queried in a straightforward way: have we had one of these previously? How many like this have happened? Second, they are analysed statistically: is there more of this kind of crime this year than last year? Are our response times acceptable, and are they improving? More subtle analysis has not, in general, been attempted because of the complexity of analysing semi-structured data where the attributes are so heterogeneous. The thrust of this chapter is that the inductive use of such data is much more powerful than conventional approaches. Instead of querying the data, clustering makes it possible to extract information from the data that indicates what general structures are present, and perhaps where there are unexpected local structures that suggest investigative targets. Many police forces are making their RMS data available on public sites (www.policedatainitiative.org/datasets/), which suggests that they believe that these data sets contain value. At the same time, making the data available implicitly conveys that they do not believe that they have the expertise to analyse them and extract their value in-house. The data sets available online are also much less rich than the one on which this chapter is based, perhaps because police departments are concerned about privacy issues and de-anonymisation.

This article begins by surveying the state of the art for leveraging data to enhance policing. The second section shows how the order-preserving hashing technique can be applied to a data set. The results show that this technique makes it possible to ascertain, empirically, responses to key questions that are commonly raised about policing, such as law enforcement performance along dimensions such as lack of social bias, lack of regional bias, and expected and appropriate responses to the problems with which it is presented. One emergent property that may repay further study is the role of apartment buildings in the landscape of certain types of crime. There was also interest in whether calls could be categorised as mental health related in advance, so that appropriate dispatch responses could be deployed, and the results suggest that this is possible.

The subsequent section analyses social networks of co-presence at the same incident. The qualitative view of the social network of criminals – at least those who come to the attention of law enforcement – that emerges suggests an absence of highly organised groups with a strategic approach to their criminality. This too is a significant finding in terms of appropriate intervention and prevention strategies. The conclusion then sums up these findings as a function of the value-added by these two techniques to analysing police RMS incident data and gauges the broader validity of the findings.

State of the art

Data analytics is an emerging tool for law enforcement. Police already rely widely on gathering and analysing data digitally. For example, most departments have an electronic system for recording an officer's notes or calls to a tip line. Often, critical data such as the time, place, type of crime, and witness details are captured (Nath, 2006). These notes are often collections of data that a police officer uses to draw inferences about an offender. Police commonly have a system in place to record this information electronically. Many departments use these RMS only as a way of archiving data. However, police are becoming increasingly cognisant of the analytic opportunities such data enable.

Data analytics can take many forms: entity extraction, clustering techniques, rule mining, classification, and social network analysis, for instance. Clustering can be used to find similarities among groups of criminals, groups of crime occurrences, and times and locations where incidents happen. Police departments that use clustering techniques can 'identify suspects who commit crimes in similar ways or distinguish among groups belonging to different gangs' (Chen et al., 2004, p. 51), generalising the modus operandi files that police have used for more than a century. Police departments can also develop predictive models that suggest locations, times, or situations that have elevated risks for crime occurrence. The use of data analytic techniques has two principal advantages that complement the experience of officers: they demonstrably avoid bias (both social and cognitive), and they are measurably more accurate, increasing effectiveness. Sometimes, data analytics can identify patterns of which police were unaware. In its strong form, this has precipitated a shift toward what has commonly become known as 'predictive policing'. In a weaker form, knowing these patterns can suggest new investigative directions that are likely to be productive.

Handling incident data within an analytic framework also helps make connections between current and previous crime patterns which may be known to officers but are easily missed because of shift turnover (in the short term) and employee turnover (in the medium term). A passive RMS system preserves this information, but officers must actively look for it; an analytic system can 'push' potentially useful patterns to officers.

Hot spot policing

Geography is also a critical component of many patterns of crime. A method known as 'hot spot' policing allows law enforcement to identify where offences tend to be concentrated. Hot spots are identified by plotting the historical patterns of previous incidents. When these plots show clusters – geographically close incidents – these are called hot spots (Nath, 2006). They suggest locations where proactive deployment can suppress potential crimes. Hot spot policing is defined as the practice of 'policing focused on small geographic places or areas where crime in concentrated' (Koper, 2014, p. 123). Identifying areas of crime through computerised aggregates of data dates back to the 1970s (McEwen & Taxman, 1995). Hot spot policing has since emerged as one of the most critical innovations in the policing (Koper, 2014).

Information on hot spots allows police to optimise the geographic allocation of scarce resources and skills. In an effort to reinforce the 'policing by consent' approach, a hot spot might benefit from greater police visibility and the form that visibility should take, such as police interaction with civilians rather than patrol. When Bill Bratton (2011) was chief of the Los Angeles Police Department, using a data-enabled approach to policing reduced crime in certain areas merely by having police engage more with the community. The presence of competent, sophisticated community-oriented policing heightened the community's confidence that offenders would be apprehended and held responsible for their crimes. Concentrating officers in areas identified as having higher incidence of crime than others (also known as 'cops on the dots'), Los Angeles experienced a consistent reduction in crime over seven consecutive years. Rather than being merely reactive, police can concentrate their analytical and diplomatic efforts on resolving underlying issues proactively in a hot spot for which crime may merely be a symptom (Koper, 2014).

The sites of burglaries, for example, are more likely to be burgled again. Bernasco found that scholars such as Johnson et al. (2007) concluded that 'in the wake of a domestic burglary, not only the property itself but also properties near the victimised property have an elevated burglary risk' (Bernasco, 2008, p. 412). The risk of a repeat burglary can remain heightened for at least a month. If burgled homes are at an increased risk of re-victimisation, then police can 'harden' the target by increasing their presence around such properties (Bowers & Johnson, 2004). Hardening the target can also include identifying individual characteristics that make the dwelling or the victim susceptible to theft. Research indicates that the same offenders are likely to burgle the same dwelling again and often with the same *modus operandi* (Bernasco, 2008).

Less obviously, researchers have shown that the social networks of, and around, criminals have their own hot spots. The distribution of gunshot victims is much more likely in the social network of those who have been arrested, and even within such social networks is highly skewed (Papachristos et al., 2015). If police can identify those regions of criminal social networks that have the highest risk of violence, they can begin to be proactive about pre-empting such violence.

Hot spot policing has thus established itself an innovative approach to identifying areas with substantial crime so resources can be allocated accordingly. This approach is predicated on the assumption that crime is not randomly distributed. Statistics indicate that areas that have experienced crime are more likely to be the location of future crime. Studies across US cities have shown that 5 percent of addresses tend to be associated with half of a city's crime (Koper, 2014).

Intelligence is key to reducing crime successfully among repeat offenders. It is well established that a small portion of the population is disproportionally responsible for the majority of crime (e.g., Wolfgang, Figlio, & Sellin, 1972). Versteegh, Van Der Plas, and Nieuwstraten (2013) found that in 2002 '85% of these very active repeat offenders still reoffended in the same year. In 2006, that share dropped to 70%, after which the share of reoffending repeat offenders rose slightly to 77% in 2008' (p. 72). Intelligence helps identify prolific offenders and promotes activities that will deter them from offending.

For those who are not deterred, vigilance heightens the likelihood of their arrest should they offend (Groff et al., 2015). In a controlled experiment by the Philadelphia Police Department that targeted prolific offenders, locations with an offender-focused approach saw a 50 percent reduction in violent felonies (Groff et al., 2015).

Hot spot policing thus has a track-record of reducing crime. Bratton (2011) squarely attributes part of that reduction to the role of hot spots play in predictive policing. Adding more police to a high-crime area deters crime: 'with no criminal act, there was no arrest, no conviction, and no incarceration of perpetrators' (p. 66). Also, the community feels more secure, knowing that perpetrators are more likely to be identified and caught. Statistically, other cities that practise hot spot policing also saw a reduction in crime, sometimes by 80 percent (Braga, Papachristos, & Hureau, 2014).

Larger police departments usually have greater discretion to allocate resources and analytical tools to hot spot policing. A study of hot spot policing across 198 agencies found that the practice is employed disproportionately by larger jurisdictions (Koper, 2014). Departments that did not participate tended to be smaller, with fewer than 100,000 residents. They may not have capacity, but they may also feel that there are diminishing returns on hot spot policing in smaller communities. We deliberately picked a smaller community for this exploratory study, in part, to investigate this.

Method

This article introduces two methods not currently commonly used by police: a combination of order-preserving hashing that allows attributes of many different kinds to be made comparable and a clustering technique based on singular value decomposition that allows similarities and differences among incidents to be detected and visualised. Second, social networks based on co-presence at incidents are constructed and embedded, allowing a different kind of structural similarity to be visualised.

First, an order-preserving hashing technique, developed by the authors, was applied to the incident records, converting them into records whose attributes were entirely numeric. This deals with attributes such as addresses, names, crime codes, and so on, in a consistent way. The resulting data was clustered using singular value decomposition, enabling them to be visualised in a three-dimensional space in which closeness accurately represents similarity. In such visualisations, therefore, incident records that are globally similar are placed close to one another, enabling clusters and other kinds of structures to be detected. Incident records also contain geographical coordinates, enabling attribute values to be overlaid on a map of Kingston, so that patterns associated with locations can also be visualised.

Second, the social network corresponding to co-presence at an incident was constructed from the incident records. Each node in this graph corresponds to an individual; weighted edges between each pair of individuals records how often both were present at the same incident during 2015. Since a total of 30,654 individuals were involved in incidents, these data were thresholded to select only those who appear frequently. Versions of this social network with different thresholds were embedded using a technique called spectral embedding. This places nodes (corresponding to individuals) at positions that reflect their closeness, via weighted edges, in the entire social network, and so enable their significance to be seen directly in the visualisation. Thus, spectral embedding is the social network analogue of singular value decomposition clustering. Other properties can be overlaid on these visualisations; in particular, we label each node by how often each individual was arrested at any of the incidents during the year.

Results

We first present the results obtained by clustering the incident records, followed by results from the social networks. We examine six different perspectives on the global similarity of incident records:

1 Similarity among all incident records, including those that do not involve a crime, and where the interaction with police is at the police station;
2 Similarity with respect to administrative attributes, that is the way in which police respond to incidents (for example, matching the response to the apparent kind and severity of an incident);
3 Similarity with respect to geography, exploring whether different regions of the city are served differentially;
4 Distinctions between mental health incidents and all others, hinting that predictive models could be built to guide responding officers;
5 Similarity among incident records associated with actual crimes (rather than the large number of interactions with the public where no actual crime has occurred); and
6 Similarity among incident records where response was deemed to require a high priority response.

Some of these perspectives inform the relationship between police and city (are police unbiased?), while others inform police performance on their own terms (are dispatches appropriate to the nature of a call?).

Similarity among all incident records

Attributes associated with dates were eliminated since they only introduce a gradient across the incident records for the year. The basic clustering of all incident records is shown in Figure 5.1.

Figure 5.1 contains one point for each incident record; records are close to one another when they are similar; and therefore, the visible structure indicates that there are (at least) three significant clusters: one to the left; one down and to the right; and one up and to the right. This is global similarity, calculated across all of the attributes

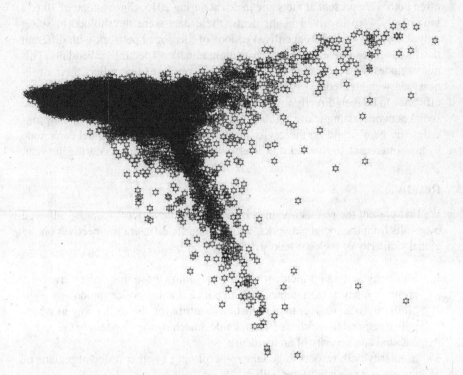

Figure 5.1 Global similarity among RMS incident records

of all records. Typical records will be placed centrally (because they resemble other typical records), and so the most unusual records are placed extremally.

A greater benefit comes from understanding what these clusters represent: why a particular incident record lies in a particular place. To achieve this, the basic clustering can be overlaid with greyscale coding based on the values of any single attribute, with the shading representing the magnitudes of the values. Thus, an attribute that has no correlation with the global similarity structure will produce an image where the grey variation is randomly distributed, while an attribute that is associated with the structure of the global clustering will have regions of light or dark.

The meaning of this clustering can be seen most directly by considering the overlay of RUCR codes, as shown in Figure 5.2.

Larger values of these codes correspond to general information and vehicle reports; lower numbers to more serious crimes. Thus, we conclude that serious crimes are associated with the two long arms, while lesser crimes and routine interactions between police and citizens are associated with the left-hand arm/cluster.

Further understanding of the clusters comes from overlaying attributes such as object-of-theft1 (a theft of a single object) which shows that the downward cluster is associated with crimes such as thefts. Overlaying the attribute object-of-theft2 (a theft of two objects) shows that the incidents lower in the arm (i.e., more extremal) are associated with more complex thefts (Figures 5.3 and 5.4).

rucr

Figure 5.2 Crime codes (RUCR) overlaid on global similarity

object-of-theft2

Figure 5.3 Overlay of thefts involving two or more objects

object-of-theft1

Figure 5.4 Overlay of all thefts

Overlaying the offence attribute shows that there is an association between the offence committed and all of the other attributes of each record. The cluster up and to the right contains incidents involving multiple offences. Points furthest to the right are associated with four or five offences in a single incident (Figure 5.5).

Weapon status shows a similar pattern – incidents involving weapons are associated with the top right-hand cluster (Figure 5.6).

Administrative attributes

The relationship between temporal properties and incidents, especially violent incidents, can also be detected from the clustering.

We first show the clustering overlaid by day of the week in Figure 5.7. The relationship is at best weak – perhaps the shading distribution in the upper right arm is slightly different to the rest of the figure. Hence there is little difference in the pattern of incidents occurring on different week days.

The overlay of time of day can also be computed. Here there is a temporal pattern – the darker central points correspond to apparently minor crime-related incidents that occur at a particular time of day (Figure 5.8).

Other administrative associations in the clustering can also be observed. The founded attribute is associated with what investigating officers conclude were

offence

Figure 5.5 Overlay of offence codes

weapon-status

Figure 5.6 Overlay of offences involving weapons

week-day

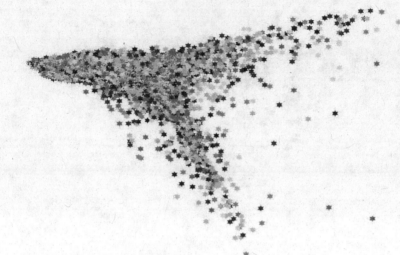

Figure 5.7 Overlay of day of the week

occ-time

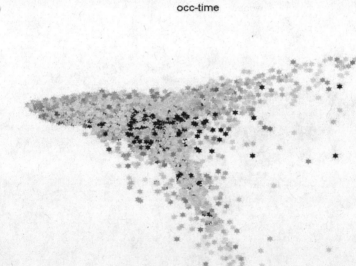

Figure 5.8 Overlay of time of day for each incident

Figure 5.9 Crime clearance for each incident

actual crimes. Figure 5.9 shows that these appear in the two right-hand arms; those in the left-hand arm are either reports for which an actual crime cannot be identified or incidents not associated with a crime, such as vehicle accidents.

The overlap of unit-id1 (identifying the first unit dispatched to an incident) (Figure 5.10) shows that there is no dispatch for many thefts.

Similarly, priority (Figure 5.11) is associated with the extremal incidents to the upper right and lower left, showing that dispatchers are appropriately prioritising incidents involving more serious crimes. The small dark clusters represent the records associated with reporting traffic accidents.

Of particular interest is the ability to recognise mental-health incidents, preferably before officers arrive at the incident. A mental-health attribute was constructed from the existing data using appropriate RUCR codes; the result is shown in Figure 5.12.

The incidents for which the mental health attribute applies form a tight cluster, tighter than the clusters associated with other kinds of incidents, and so are clearly similar in other ways than simply how they are coded after the fact. This offers the potential to build a predictive model that could warn responders when they are dispatched to a possible mental health call.

Geographical distribution

We now consider the overlaying of attributes on a geographical rendering of Kingston, since each incident is geotagged. The following figures show that there is no bias or preference in service based on region within Kingston.

unit-id1

Figure 5.10 First unit dispatched to each incident

priority

Figure 5.11 Priority of dispatch for each incident

mental-health

Figure 5.12 Incidents involving mental health are globally similar

The case-class overlay (Figure 5.13) shows that crimes are distributed uniformly across the region, although there are (not surprisingly) small, local tendencies to clump.

Similarly, the distribution by day of the week and by time of day (Figures 5.14 and 5.15) shows no strong patterns.

Priority of response (Figure 5.16) also shows no geographical patterns, so there is no *a priori* bias to service particular areas.

Complainant sex and date of birth (Figures 5.17 and 5.18) also show no indication of bias along these lines by region of the city.

These results demonstrate, empirically, that the Kingston Police deals with incidents and locations in a fair and unbiased manner. The ability to demonstrate, empirically, that police forces are responding appropriately is an important benefit of this approach, allowing forces to demonstrate to their oversight bodies, and the general public, that they are performing well.

Focusing on criminal incidents

The full range of incidents includes many that are not associated with crimes. A clustering using a smaller number of attributes, focusing mainly on crimes themselves, has a similar structure, but patterns associated with thefts and violence become clearer.Figure 5.19 Global similarity among incidents involving crimes

case-class

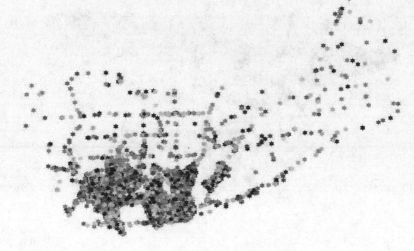

Figure 5.13 Type of incident overlaid on Kingston's geography

week-day

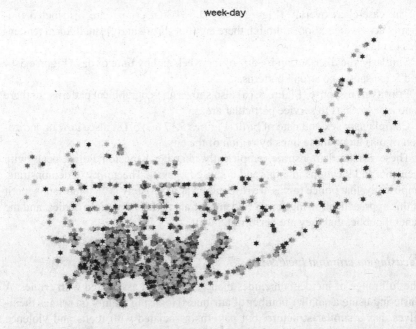

Figure 5.14 Incident day and time overlaid on geography

at-scene-time

Figure 5.15 Response time to incidents overlaid on geography

priority

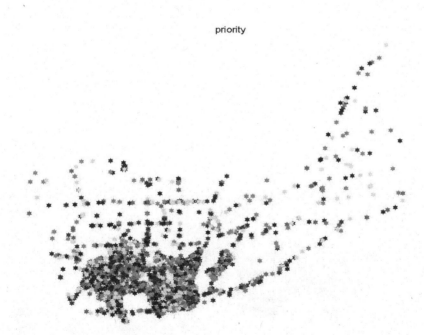

Figure 5.16 Priority overlaid on geography

comp-sex

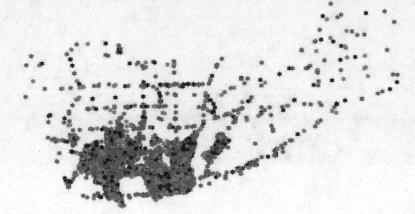

Figure 5.17 Complainant sex overlaid on geography

comp-dob

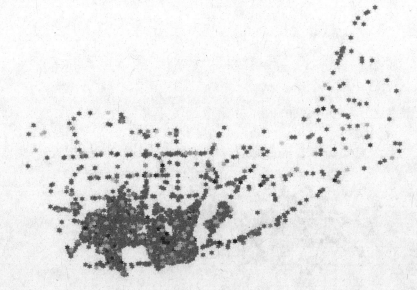

Figure 5.18 Complainant age overlaid on geography

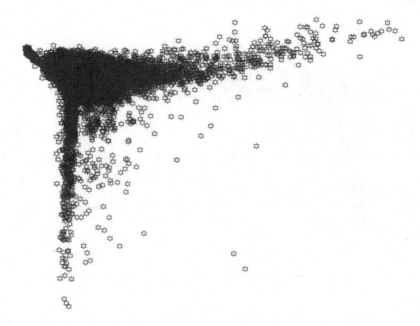

Figure 5.19 Global similarity among incidents involving crimes

The view in Figure 5.19 corresponds to a view of the previous clustering from its right-hand side: the lower arm corresponds to thefts, the right-hand arm corresponds to complex incidents, with the other previously seen structures occluded into the plane of the image. From this view, two properties are apparent. First, there is a strong association between incidents with weapons, incidents with multiple charges, and incidents with multiple unit responses (Figures 5.20–5.22) which is expected but shows that appropriate dispatch decisions are being made.

Second, some apartments are disproportionately involved in incidents of theft and violence (Figure 5.23). There are points corresponding to apartment incidents down and to the right compared to other incidents in the same general part of the figure, and there are relatively more of them in the violent incident arm. Since apartment numbers are included in the data, it is also possible to conclude that the apartments that are disproportionately involved are those with low numbers. They are thus either in smaller buildings (which predominate in higher crime regions of the city) or they are more accessible (criminals prefer not to access the higher floors of high-rise buildings). That multiple incidents of theft are concentrated for some apartments is a finding that is consistent with the literature.

Focusing on priority 1 incidents

We also consider the clustering of incidents associated with priority 1 calls only, that is not just crimes, but crimes with an element of urgency. As expected, many

weapon-status

Figure 5.20 Crime incidents where weapons were used

unit-id2

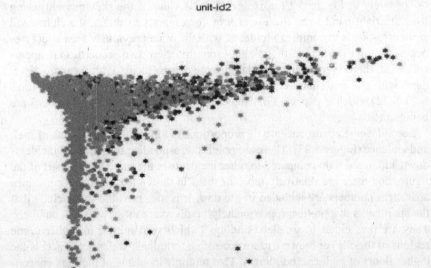

Figure 5.21 Crime incidents where more than one unit was dispatched

offence2

Figure 5.22 Crime incidents where more than one crime took place

apartment

Figure 5.23 Crime incidents involving apartments

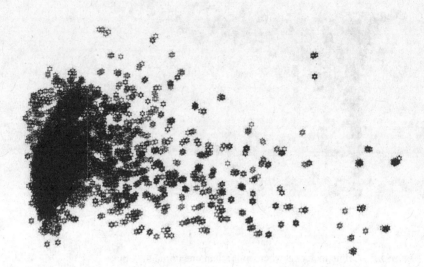

Figure 5.24 Global similarity among incidents classed as priority 1

more these incidents are associated with violence. The basic clustering is shown in Figure 5.24.

Points further to the right are associated with increasing number of offences, increasing number of non-null RUCR values, and weapon attributes. Incidents involving thefts tends to be on the upper side, with the more complex ones toward the upper right (Figures 5.25 and 5.26).

Many incidents require multiple units to be dispatched (Figures 5.27 and 5.28).

There is a strong association between family violence, apartments, and time of day, shown in Figures 5.29–5.31. Note that this association is with low-numbered apartments (coloured darker), which is a surrogate for non-high-rise accommodation.

These results show the potential of our hashing + clustering approach to reveal both empirically supported performance data, and useful intelligence from routine RMS data.

Social networks built from co-presence

We now turn to the social networks whose links are built from co-presence at the same incident. Co-offending networks have been studied extensively as a way of understanding the pathways that cause criminals to choose to commit crimes in pairs or larger groups. That there are other individuals in the environment of criminals who also play a role in the dynamics of criminal group crime is less apparent. Family or relatives, ethnic kin, and elites are well-established enablers

Figure 5.25 Thefts overlaid on priority 1 calls

offence

Figure 5.26 Number of offences overlaid on priority 1 calls

unit-id2

Figure 5.27 Incidents where at least two units were dispatched on priority 1 calls

unit-id3

Figure 5.28 Incidents where at least three units were dispatched on priority 1 calls

family-violence

Figure 5.29 Family violence overlaid on priority 1 calls

time-received

Figure 5.30 Time of day overlaid on priority 1 calls

apartment

Figure 5.31 Location at an apartment overlaid with priority 1 calls

of illicit networks (Magouirk, Atran, & Sageman, 2008; Sheffer, 2005; Sageman, 2004; Massey, Ceballos, Espinosa, Palloni, & Spittel, 2001). For example, family membership may increase the trust between a pair of potentially co-offending criminals, and their connection may be mediated by an innocent, non-criminal family member. Similarly, the distribution of victims is also not random – a victim may be chosen because of previous knowledge gained via some other social relationship or proximity. A social network of co-offenders may thus represent the immediate functional connections among criminals, but its structure depends on a wider social network that includes other individuals such as relatives, acquaintances, and those in physical proximity to the actual criminals.

Each incident record in the RMS data contains a numeric identifier for each individual concerned, including those charged, victims and witnesses. We create a co-presence social network whose nodes represent each individual who appears in the data. Two individuals are involved in the same incident generate an edge between them in the social network. When three individuals are concerned, edges are generated between all pairs, and so on. The result is a graph whose nodes represent individuals, with edges weighted by the number of incidents at which they both were present.

Figure 5.32 shows a histogram of the number of incidents groups of individuals are involved in during this one-year period. About 11,000 individuals are involved in an incident with only one other person, about 6000 are involved with

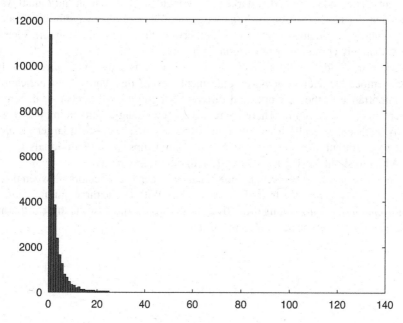

Figure 5.32 Histogram of the number of interactions with police in a single year

two other people (either in two separate incidents, or with two others in a single incident), and so on. It is noteworthy how skewed this distribution is (and the close agreement with Price's Law) which is again reassuring about the normal operation of Kingston Police. The highest level of involvement by a single individual is 136 – interacting with police more than twice a week.

The interesting part of this co-presence social network is the core region, containing the individuals who both interact most often with law enforcement, and with one another. The following figures show the embedding of the core component (the largest connected subgroup) when thresholds of 40, 30, and 10 incidents per year are used to select individuals. In other words, with threshold t, only those individuals whose weighted degree in the social network was at least t are considered. Degree combines number of interactions with number of other individuals involved. For example, an individual involved in two incidents with the same other person, two incidents with a different person each time, or a single incident with two others would all have degree two.

Note that, because this social network is based only on encounters with law enforcement, we cannot determine the true underlying social network of these individuals. We see only that part of their relationship structure that intersects with drawing attention from police. These social networks are, therefore, limited compared to those that might be developed by a full intelligence analysis; but they are much cheaper to create, since the data required is already available in RMS systems. The nodes are coded darker if any incident in which an individual was involved during 2015 resulted in a charge and the size of the symbol indicates how many such incidents there were; otherwise they are coded lighter. Such a node typically corresponds to a victim or a witness.

With threshold 40, 150 individuals are involved, as shown in Figure 5.33. In these embedded social networks, placement toward the centre is an indication of importance in the network, and different subgroups will appear in different directions from the centre. There are relatively few triangles, indicating that these individuals are typically involved in incidents in pairs, rather than larger groups. The long straight lines indicate chain-like relationships among individuals.

With threshold 30 (Figure 5.34), 272 individuals are involved.

There are now a set of five key individuals who act as connectors between three distinct sub-branches (the triangle in the centre). Without the three mutually inter-connected individuals among these five, the groups captured by the three different branches would not be as well connected.

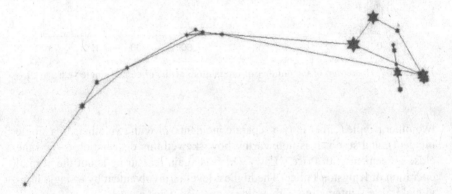

Figure 5.33 Co-presence network of those involved with police at least 40 times in a year

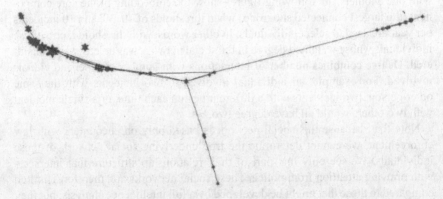

Figure 5.34 Co-presence networks of those involved with police at least 30 times in a year

Note, in the lower branch, two individuals who must often be involved in the same incidents to be placed so close together; but also note that this branch is a chain of pairwise overlapping presence at incidents.

For the first time, someone not charged with an offence during 2015 appears in the social network (a lighter point on the right-hand branch). Such a person was involved in at least 30 incidents with a number of people who were charged, without being charged themselves. Thus, such a person is of considerable interest as an unusual common factor. Such a person might be an innocent family member of a family with many criminals, or someone victimised by two different, active criminals; but it is worth noting that a police informer might also appear as such a lighter point, and police need to take the possibility into account that such people might become more detectable in this kind of analysis.

The structure of this network shows that the criminal network in Kingston (at least from this perspective) is not a spider web with a 'criminal mastermind' at the centre. Rather there are groupings of individuals who connect to one another in a loose way, with some of the connections involving individuals whose interactions with the police involve low-level issues, rather than major crimes.

Finally, zooming in to the centre of the social network with a threshold of 10 (Figure 5.35) shows the complexity of the network connecting moderately active criminals in Kingston; but at the same time emphasises how interconnected to one another these 1,904 individuals are. There are several lighter coloured points close to the centre of this network, and all of these deserve

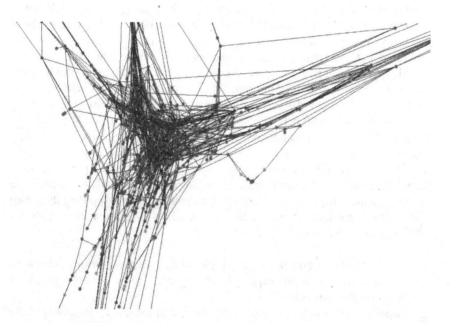

Figure 5.35 Centre of the co-presence network of those involved with police at least 10 times in a year

further attention as already mentioned – they have frequent contact with police but are never charged.

Overall, most interactions with law enforcement involve the presence of only two individuals at an incident; there are few groups of three or four (this supports previous observations that triangles in criminal social networks are much rarer than in mainstream social networks). The most active 200–300 criminals are involved in groups of moderate size, but these groups are connected to other groups by mutual participation in activities that draw attention from law enforcement (rather than competing with each other). The next tier of activity (those who are seen at fewer incidents in the course of a year) creates a complex network of interactions that is still primarily pairwise, with no indication of an organised structure. Individuals who are central, especially in the high-threshold network, both consume inordinate amounts of police time, and act as connectors between disparate subgroups. Finding ways to deal with them more effectively would produce a disproportionately beneficial improvement in the local environment.

Conclusion

This project applied two different cutting-edge techniques to analyse data from 46,668 incident records, with 188 attributes associated with each record, collected over the course of 2015 in the RMS of police in Kingston, Ontario, Canada. While this research is substantial in the way that it is the first project to analyse this data using an order-preserving hashing technique, it is inherently exploratory and its conclusions thus preliminary as it is limited to a single year of data. However, because it comprises the entire universe of the data set, the findings are reasonably robust. There are no comparable studies that apply these two techniques to police RMS data; so, we cannot gauge the validity of the findings that way. However, a study of hot spot policing found that while a month was not a reliable timeframe for data, collecting data for one year increased the accuracy of the predictions to 90 percent (Spelman, 1995). Studies of hot spot policing have also shown that some hot spots remain consistent over a large span of time (Adams-Fuller, 2001). Although they differ in technique, these observations give us a degree of confidence that results generated by the hashing plus clustering technique as well as the application of social network analysis to co-presence are likely to be detecting useful structures and relationships. Applying these two techniques to the incident record data collected by Kingston Police generates patterns that can be used to:

1   Show empirically how the force is performing, in terms of lack of social bias, lack of regional bias, and expected and appropriate responses to the problems with which it is presented;
2   Suggest issues that may repay further, more detailed study – for example, the role that apartments play in the landscape of criminal activity, and the similarity among what turn out to be mental-health calls; and,

3   Provide a qualitative view of the social network of criminals (at least those who come to the attention of law enforcement), that suggests an absence of highly organised groups with a strategic approach to their criminality.

This approach has great potential because one large prerequisite, the collection of high-quality data, is already done routinely by police forces and embedded in their RMS systems. Furthermore, only a few RMS systems, such as NICHE, are in common use; so, the analytic process can be readily generated between police forces, and properly comparable models produced.

The key impediments to wider use of this approach at present are:

1   Whether inductive analysis of data can produce actionable intelligence: most users of data are used to an interrogative model, where questions can be asked of the data, but are unfamiliar with the idea that the data can not only generate questions it has not occurred to them to ask but also to provide answers to such questions;

2   Reticence that the results of inductive analysis could be misused to make consequential decisions (as suggested in the film *Minority Report*, for example). The results can, however, be used to respond better to the highly skewed distribution of crimes by location, type, and criminals; and

3   Lack of the skillsets in police departments to appreciate and perform the kind of inductive analysis illustrated in this chapter. It is difficult to embed these techniques in off-the-shelf packages, since some level of understanding is required to interpret the results of clusterings as they inform operational decision making.

Importantly, these impediments can be overcome; and the payoffs from intelligence-led policing are so compelling that we expect to see variants of data analytics showcased in this chapter penetrating police departments quite rapidly.

References

Adams-Fuller, T. (2001). *Historical homicide hot spots: The case of three cities* (Doctoral dissertation). Howard University, Washington, DC.

Bernasco, W. (2008). Them again? Same-offender involvement in repeat and near repeat burglaries. *European Journal of Criminology, 5*(4), 411–431.

Braga, A. A., Papachristos, A. V., & Hureau, D. M. (2014). The effects of hot spots policing on crime: Updated systematic review and meta-analysis. *Justice Quarterly, 31*(4), 633–663.

Bratton, W. J. (2011). Reducing crime through prevention not incarceration. *Criminology & Public Policy, 10*(1), 63–68.

Bowers, K. J., & Johnson, S. D. (2004). Who commits near repeats? A test of the boost explanation. *Western Criminology Review, 5*(3), 12–24.

Chen, H., Chung, W., Xu, J. J., Wang, G., Qin, Y., & Chau, M. (2004). Crime data mining: A general framework and some examples. *Computer, 37*(4), 50–56.

Groff, E. R., Ratcliffe, J. H., Haberman, C. P., Sorg, E. T., Joyce, N. M., & Taylor, R. B. (2015). Does what police do at hot spots matter? The Philadelphia policing tactics experiment. *Criminology, 53*(1), 23–53. doi:10.1111/1745-9125.12055

Johnson, S. D., Bernasco, W., Bowers, K., Elffers, H., Ratcliffe, J., Rengert, G., & Townsley, M. (2007). Space-time patterns of risk: A cross national assessment of residential burglary victimization. *Journal of Quantitative Criminology, 23*(3), 201–219.

Koper, C. S. (2014). Assessing the practice of hot spots policing: Survey results from a national convenience sample of local police agencies. *Journal of Contemporary Criminal Justice, 30*(2), 123–146. doi:10.1177/1043986214525079

Magouirk, J., Atran, S., & Sageman, M. (2008). Connecting terrorist networks. *Studies in Conflict & Terrorism, 31*(1), 1–16.

Massey, D., Ceballos, M., Espinosa, K., Palloni, A., & Spittel, M. (2001). Social capital and international migration: A test using information on family networks. *American Journal of Sociology, 106*(4), 1262–1299.

McEwen, J. T., & Taxman, F. S. (1995). Applications of computer mapping to police operations. In J. E. Eck & D. Weisburd (Eds.), *Crime and place* (Crime Prevention Studies, Vol. 4, pp. 259–284). Monsey, NY: Criminal Justice Press.

Morselli, C. (2014). *Crime and networks*. Abingdon: Routledge.

Nath, S. V. (2006). Crime pattern detection using data mining. *2006 IEEE/WIC/ACM International Conference on Web Intelligence and Intelligent Agent Technology Workshops, 2006, WI-IAT 2006 Workshops*, 41–44, IEEE.

Papachristos, A. V., Braga, A. A., Piza, E., & Grossman, L. S. (2015). The company you keep? The spillover effects of gang membership on individual gunshot victimization in a co-offending network. *Criminology, 53*(4), 624–649.

Sageman, M. (2004). *Understanding terrorist networks*. Philadelphia: University of Pennsylvania Press.

Sheffer, G. (2005). Diasporas, terrorism and WMD. *International Studies Review, 7*(1), 133–170.

Spelman, W. (1995). Criminal careers of public places. In D. Weisburd & J. Eck (Eds.), *Crime and place* (Crime Prevention Studies, Vol. 4, pp. 115–144). Monsey, NY: Criminal Justice Press.

Versteegh, P., Van Der Plas, T., & Nieuwstraten, H. (2013). The best of three worlds: More effective policing by a problem-oriented approach of hot crimes, hot spots, hot shots, and hot groups. *Police Practice and Research, 14*(1), 66–81.

Wolfgang, M., Figlio, R., & Sellin, T. (1972). *Delinquency in a birth cohort*. Chicago: University of Chicago Press.

6 The challenges and concerns of using big data to understand cybercrime

Jin Ree Lee and Thomas J. Holt

Introduction

The proliferation of computers, mobile devices, and the internet have revolution-ised all aspects of modern life. Traditional boundaries of space and time have been rendered meaningless, as individuals can interact in real time through text or instant messaging, as well as asynchronously via email, forums, and other forms of computer-mediated communications (Holt & Bossler, 2016; Newman & Clarke, 2003; Wall, 2001). Individuals are also no longer limited to either writ-ten or voice messaging, as decentralised social networking sites like Facebook, Instagram, and Snapchat enable users to share content using any combination of text, images, and video (Holt & Bossler, 2016). The internet has also changed the landscape of financial transactions and commerce, making it possible for people to buy goods and services from vendors around the world. Retailers maintain cus-tomers' financial data in large databases, enabling payments to be made instantly via various currencies (Holt & Bossler, 2016).

Given the relative ease with which individuals can access the internet across various devices, most nations are now dependent on technology for critical ser-vices (Andress & Winterfeld, 2013; Holt & Bossler, 2016; Newman & Clarke, 2003). These benefits have also created unparalleled opportunities for individu-als to misuse online resources to engage in a variety of deviant and criminal acts (Holt & Bossler, 2016). A new lexicon has developed to define the scope of these offenses, particularly the phrase *cybercrime*, recognising the use of the internet and/ or internet-enabled devices to perform acts of crime and deviance (Furnell, 2002; Wall, 2001). Traditional crimes that occur in real world environments have been enhanced by technology, including prostitution (Cunningham & Kendall, 2010; Holt & Blevins, 2007), fraud (Cross, 2015; Wall, 2004), stalking and harassment (Bocij, 2004; Choi & Lee, 2017; Choi, Lee, & Lee, 2017), terrorism (Britz, 2010; Weimann, 2005), piracy (Higgins & Marcum, 2011), and child sexual offenses (Jenkins, 2001; Krone, 2004). New forms of crime have also developed as a func-tion of technology, including unauthorised access of computers and the dissemina-tion of malicious software (Bossler & Holt, 2009; Jordan & Taylor, 1998).

The rise of cybercrime presents a unique challenge for academic research-ers and policy-makers, as the number of calls for service for these offenses, the

composition of offender populations, and victim characteristics are not well explicated in official data sources such as the Uniform Crime Report in the US, or the
British Crime Survey in England and Wales (Brenner, 2009; Wall, 2007). Additionally, large-scale, nationally representative self-report studies of deviance and
crime do not include measures for cybercriminality, making it difficult to understand the predictors and pathways to offending (Holt & Bossler, 2016).

Some researchers have begun to use alternative data sources as a means to
understand cybercrime, specifically text and visual information posted by individuals in clear-text through various online data sources, including websites, social
media feeds, and computer-mediated communications platforms (see Holt, 2017;
Silverman, 2013 for reviews). Offenders discuss their motivations, methods, and
target preferences on forums, Facebook, Twitter, and other sites due to the degree
of anonymity afforded by the internet. In addition, some platforms exist solely
to facilitate overt criminality, such as illicit markets operating to sell personal
information (e.g., Franklin, Paxson, Perrig, & Savage, 2007; Holt & Lampke,
2010; Hutchings & Holt, 2015), hacking tools (Dupont, Côté, Boutin, & Fernandez, 2017; Holt, 2013b), drugs (e.g., Barratt, 2012; Decary-Hetu & Quessy-Dore,
2017), and sexual services (Horswill & Weitzer, 2018; Kosloski, Bontrager-
Ryon, & Roe-Sepowitz, 2017). These sources provide deep insights at the individual and aggregate level to understand both offender perspectives and potential
targets for victimisation.

To date, most researchers have used online data collection methods to examine
cybercrimes using both qualitative and quantitative models (see Holt & Bossler,
2016 for review). While cross-sectional and longitudinal studies are useful for
examining relationships between predetermined variables, these analyses are
incapable of interpreting the associations found within individualised transactions
established in cyberspace (Song, Song, An, Hayman, & Woo, 2014). The quantity of data available through online sources, including years of text and images,
could enable big data mining and analysis techniques to assess the practices of
online offenders and their potential victims (Chen, Mao, & Liu, 2014; Clark,
2017; Song, Song, & Lee, 2018; Williams, Burnap, & Sloan, 2017). While big
data has the ability to illustrate various trends that can be later examined to support and/or challenge wider assumptions, they do not make any inferences themselves (Smith, Moses, & Chan, 2017; Song et al., 2018). The benefits of analysing
big data rests in its ability to consolidate a larger volume of data and confirm
the thoughts of a host of participants, lending itself to more accurate predictions
(Song et al., 2018; Williams et al., 2017). Additionally, though big data research
is commonplace among certain disciplines (e.g., nursing, engineering, business,
and medicine), it has not been used with much consistency in criminal justice (see
Smith et al., 2017; Williams et al., 2017).

Despite the various challenges and limitations of big data, it is a burgeoning
phenomenon that demands more attention and consideration within inquiries that
investigate cybercrime and cybersecurity. This chapter will examine the challenges and concerns of using big data within cybercrime research, beginning with
an introduction of big data and its defining characteristics. Then, we consider why

and how big data could be applied uniquely to crime, as well as perspectives on how big data could prevent the emergence of modern crime problems. The chapter will conclude with a discussion on the risks and implications posed by using big data to examine cybercrime offending and victimisation.

Big data

Big data is generally defined as enormous data sets that cannot 'be perceived, acquired, managed, and processed by traditional information technology and software/hardware tools within a tolerable time' (Chen et al., 2014, p. 173). In other words, big data is defined by the voluminous size of the rows and columns of the data within the file, its increasing scale, and its inability to be handled by conventional technologies (Williams et al., 2017; Wu, Zhu, Wu, & Ding, 2014). This description is not uniform across all stakeholders, as different actors and disciplines hold varying conceptualisations of big data based on the particular aspects they value the most (Chen et al., 2014; Smith et al., 2017).

Numerous industry sectors and fields have shown interest in the potential utility of big data. For instance, Google has been reported to processes data requests equalling hundreds of petabytes (PB) every month, while Facebook generates log data of over 10PB a month. Other companies such as Baidu, a Chinese internet-services company, have reported processing data at tens of PB per day (Chen et al., 2014). A 2011 report from the International Data Corporation (IDC) indicated that the total amount of data created and copied in the world was 1.8 zettabyte (ZB), an increase in volume of nearly nine times since 2006 (Chen et al., 2014).

If such quantities of data can be properly harnessed for analysis, substantial improvements on the productivity and competitiveness of both private and public organisations can be had, while also generating huge benefits for its consumers (Chen et al., 2014). For example, if big data could be used to its full potential by the US medical industry, it could potentially net over USD 300 billion and reduce expenditures of the US healthcare system by over eight percent (Chen et al., 2014). Private retailers that could fully utilise big data may also be able to increase their profit by more than 60 percent (Chen et al., 2014).

In order to maximise the power and potential of big data, a fundamental change in the computing architecture and large-scale data processing mechanism is needed (Chen et al., 2014). To this effect, IBM has invested over USD 16 billion on more than 30 acquisitions related to big data since 2005 (Chen et al., 2014). These acquisitions consist of procuring other companies specialising in analytics-based data processing. One such example is IBM's acquisition of Aspera in 2014 – a company specialised in securely moving massive data files around the world using fast transmission speeds. Other examples include acquiring Vivisimo (a leading provider of big data discovery and navigation) in 2012 and Cleversafe (a leading developer in big data storage) in 2015. Similarly, the Obama administration had announced a USD 200 million investment to launch the 'Big Data Research and Development Plan' in March 2012, making it the second major scientific and technological development initiative since 1993 (Chen et al., 2014).

While the advantages of big data are wide-ranging, its growth has produced many challenging obstacles that demand precise solutions. Specifically, it is imperative that analysts determine methods to ascertain values from data sets with enormous scales and rapid generation (Chen et al., 2014; Smith et al., 2017). This includes managing large quantities of unstructured data that require significant amounts of real-time-analysis. Additionally, data must be acquired from a wide pool of data sources in order to be combined for analysis (Chen et al., 2014; Williams et al., 2017). Finally, all of this information must be stored and retained with moderate requirements on hardware and software infrastructure.

Big data and traditional crime

Though many think of big data analytics as an issue for technology companies and industry, there is substantial value in operationalising big data and data mining analyses to the criminal justice system to combat modern crime problems (Chan & Moses, 2017). Police departments worldwide have begun using big data, machine learning, and predictive analytics to both understand and prevent crime, giving them the opportunity to position police resources in response to anticipated dangers (Clark, 2017). For instance, when previous arrest records are amassed with real-time internet of things (IOT) data, such as censored cameras constructed to recognise gunshots, it becomes easier for law enforcement to diagnose problem locations and understand the conditions in which crimes flourish (Clark, 2017). By applying predictive analytics and machine learning to large data sets, police departments are able to improve their ability to forecast both where and when violent crimes will emerge and ensure that they have the adequate resources in place to prevent such behaviours from occurring (Clark, 2017).

An excellent example of such a strategy is IBM's HunchLab, which is a geographic prediction tool that uses data modelling to identify various risks and dangers across specific areas (Clark, 2017). At-risk areas are marked on-screen, while suggestions for action are displayed along the side, such as dispatching a high visibility police patrol car to take control of the situation and deter criminals. This information is aggregated into a 'decision support system', made available to police officers in the field (Clark, 2017). IBM reports that this predictive approach has worked best against robberies, theft, and burglaries, as in Manchester, England, where its implementation was linked to reported reductions of robberies, burglaries, and theft from vehicles (Clark, 2017).

While tools such as HunchLab are effective on certain types of crime, it is worth noting that other crimes may be much harder to prognosticate. This could be due to the random and isolated nature of various incidents; or because their offenders operate clandestinely with the help and protection of larger organisations (Clark, 2017). In such scenarios, big data can still be used to predict the risks of crime. For example, digital traces from various online communication tools (e.g., social media, emails, webpages visited) can be analysed to predict potential attacks before they happen. A major challenge to this approach, however, is the volume of content. Not only can filtering (e.g., finding alarming content, trends, or patterns) through such data be time consuming, but the analyses can be misleading, as various online content may contain exaggerations and/or inaccuracies in meaning. Identifying whether certain items are truly predictors of crime can thus be difficult without deeper insight (Clark, 2017).

The problem of cybercrime

Though there are myriad official and secondary sources that could be used for big data aggregation and analysis of street crime, they are largely absent for cybercrimes. In fact, the term cybercrime may be somewhat confusing to the general public, as it encompasses a range of offenses affecting both property and persons. One of the most comprehensive frameworks to categorise cybercrime was developed by David Wall (2001), who argued for a four-item typology: 1) cyber-trespass, 2) cyber-deception/theft, 3) cyber-porn/obscenity, and 4) cyber-violence. Acts of cyber-trespass involve attempts to cross established boundaries of ownership in a networked environment (Wall, 2001). Trespass may originate from computer hackers who attempt to penetrate computer systems and networks they do not own or have permission to use (Holt & Bossler, 2016). Hackers may also utilise malicious software, or malware, which are programs designed to compromise computer systems and acquire sensitive information, establish backdoor access to systems, and disrupt network connectivity (Bossler & Holt, 2009; Holt & Kilger, 2012; Schell & Dodge, 2002; Symantec Corporation, 2013).

Cyber-deception and theft involve the use of fraud and deceit to acquire information, services, or funds from a target (Wall, 2001). Some of these acts are associated with acts of cyber-trespass, such as the use of hacking in order to access financial data from corporate databases or payment systems (Franklin et al., 2007; Hutchings & Holt, 2015). Cyber-deception can also include the use of mass emails, also called spam, in order to fraudulently obtain personal information or user credentials (Cross, 2015; Edelson, 2003; Holt & Graves, 2007; Nhan, Kinkade, & Burns, 2009; Wall, 2004). This category also recognises digital piracy, where individuals use file sharing software and tools to download music, movies, and other intellectual property without paying its creator or owner (Higgins & Marcum, 2011; Nhan, 2013).

The third category, cyber-porn and obscenity, references the use of technology to engage in sexual activities (Wall, 2001). Not only has the internet and digital technology made it easier for individuals to create and share pornographic content, but it also engenders sex work on and offline (Quinn & Forsyth, 2005; Roberts & Hunt, 2012; Yar, 2013). Sex workers regularly use websites and forums as a means to connect with customers, negotiate payments, and complete assignations with minimal risk of detection by law enforcement (Cunningham & Kendall, 2010; Holt & Blevins, 2007; Horswill & Weitzer, 2018; Milrod & Monto, 2012). Additionally, technology has enabled the sexual exploitation of minors through online communications channels to groom children, share digital images and video of children engaged in sexual acts (IWF, 2016), and increasingly stream sexual abuse live via online platforms like Snapchat, Skype, and FaceTime (Durkin & Bryant, 1999; GSMA, 2014; Krone, 2004).

The final category includes acts of cyber-violence, which involves the use of digital technology to solicit, create, and distribute physically and/or emotionally damaging information to harm individuals (Wall, 2001). For instance, individuals now use text messages, social media, and email as vehicles to harass or stalk individuals (Bocij, 2004; Hinduja & Patchin, 2014; Reyns, Henson, & Fisher, 2012). Online communications platforms are also frequently used by extremist groups and terrorists to recruit new members to the movement, as well as issue threats against wide audiences based on race, gender, religious affiliation, and/or sexual orientation (Awan & Zempi, 2017; Britz, 2010; Yar, 2013).

Big data techniques applied to cybercrime

The diverse range of cybercrimes poses a challenge for researchers to understand the practices of offenders and risk factors associated with victimisation. However, the sheer quantity of data available from online sources provides a uniquely massive source of data that could be leveraged to examine these crimes. Utilising web scraping tools to capture posts made in various online communications platforms, including internet relay chat (IRC) forums, blogs, and social media (e.g., Holt, 2010; Maratea, 2011; Quinn & Forsyth, 2005), could generate years of data with massive user populations for analysis. A number of computer scientists have begun to employ such techniques to analyse the practices of hackers and model online communications (see Benjamin, Samtani, & Chen, 2016; Holt & Bossler, 2016). Their findings do not, however, provide substantive depth on the human aspects of these offenses, limiting their potential value to understanding the social aspects of cybercrime. Thus, we will discuss the existing literature surrounding the use of online communications for qualitative and quantitative analyses and its potential utility for big data research. We will also consider existing research that has used these sources to demonstrate their empirical value.

Forums, bulletin boards, and newsgroups

One of the most common computer-mediated communications (CMCs) that has been mined for criminological inquiry are forums (see Blevins & Holt, 2009; Holt & Blevins, 2007; Holt, Blevins, & Kuhns, 2008; Holt & Lampke, 2010; Hutchings & Holt, 2015; Motoyama, McCoy, Levchenko, Savage, & Voelker, 2011; Mann & Sutton, 1998; Malesky & Ennis, 2004; Williams & Copes, 2005; Yip, Webber, & Shadbolt, 2013), bulletin board systems (BBSs) (Jenkins, 2001; Meyer, 1989), and newsgroups (Durkin & Bryant, 1999; Gauthier & Forsyth, 1999; Loper, 2000). All forms of these CMCs allow individuals to interact in an asynchronous fashion, ranging from near real-time to years between posts.

All of these platforms are organised around a topic with discussions centred on a given issue of interest to a particular audience. For instance, a single hacking-related forum could have multiple sub-forums related to hardware hacking, software, programming/coding, and mobile platforms (e.g., Dupont et al., 2017). Additionally, they are typically populated by threads, or strings, which begin when individuals create a post to ask questions or give opinions. Individual users can then respond with their own posts, which are threaded or connected together to create a singular discussion. A thread or string may be active for years depending on the prominence of the topic within the community (e.g., Holt, 2010, 2013a).

The longevity of discussions, coupled with the relatively natural flow of conversation between the participants, led Mann and Sutton (1998) to argue that forums constitute 'a kind of marathon focused discussion group' (p. 210). The content of posts within threads and the social interactions between participants provide an excellent framework to understand the social organisation practices of offender communities (e.g., Decary-Hetu & Dupont, 2012; Dupont et al., 2017; Holt, 2013b), subcultural norms of deviant communities (Blevins & Holt, 2009; Holt, 2007; Jenkins, 2001; Roberts & Hunt, 2012), offender methodologies (e.g., Cooper & Harrison, 2001), and the products available in online markets for various illicit services (e.g., Barratt, 2012; Holt, 2013a; Hutchings & Holt, 2015; Milrod & Monto, 2012).

Much of the research utilising forum data is qualitative in nature, utilising smaller samples of posts collected from specific periods of time (see Holt & Bossler, 2016 for review). Quantitative scholarship has also used forum-based data to measure offender behaviour and test various hypotheses related to criminality that take place in both online and offline environments. For instance, Cunningham and Kendall (2010) used posts from 1999 to 2008 in a series of online prostitution review sites to identify patterns in the illicit sex trade within the US, including prices, sex acts, and the demographic composition of providers. Similarly, Decary-Hetu and Quessy-Dore (2017) examined a massive sample of cryptomarket advertisements over time to identify repeat purchases made from vendors. They found that approximately 60 percent of buyers made purchases from the same vendors, especially among those vendors who provided more information to their customers. Thus, quantitative data analyses can help inform our knowledge of trends in markets and online communities over time.

Websites, blogs, and texts

In addition to forums and BBSs, researchers have begun to use the information available in various websites as a means to understand cybercrime and deviance using both qualitative and quantitative techniques. Websites include a range of content, such as social media feeds like Facebook and Twitter, as well blogs and simple text-based pages. The content of these sites provides direct information on the thoughts of an individual in their own words through text, images, and video, as well as links to other groups and entities which share their interests (Hine, 2005). In turn, this information can be used to understand perceptions of, or attitudes toward, offending from a different perspective than the social exchanges observed in forums.

Criminological researchers have increasingly used content from webpages to understand aspects of cybercrime and offender behaviour. For instance, a study conducted by D'Ovidio and colleagues (2009) examined a sample of paedophile support forums and the content posted there to understand the ways these sites facilitate a social learning process of paedophilia (D'Ovidio, Mitman, El-Burki, & Shuman, 2009). Sociological and criminological researchers have also used data from dating sites and personal advertisements online to understand the ways that individuals solicit various partners for both traditional romantic entanglements and more deviant sexual practices (Frederick & Perrone, 2014; Grov, 2004; Tewksbury, 2003). For instance, a number of studies have explored the phenomenon of bug chasing, where HIV negative individuals actively seek out sex with HIV positive partners for the purposes of becoming infected (Grov, 2004; Tewksbury, 2003, 2006). Researchers utilised qualitative analyses of ads posted on dating sites and forums dedicated to this practice and found that individuals actively pursuing HIV infection utilised different languages to construct their ads compared to those who appeared to simply seek sexual partners.

A small number of studies have used data from blogs and social networking sites to understand self-disclosure of criminality and behaviour. Web logs, or blogs, also provide an important, though underutilised, data source in criminological research generally (Hookway, 2008). Blogs serve as a sort of electronic diary that documents individual experiences through user-generated text, video, and images which are typically listed in reverse chronological order that can be tracked over time. Many blog sites operate to allow users to make their blog as a single web page, though increasingly social networking websites, like Facebook, serve the same purpose as a blog by documenting individuals' thoughts and feelings (Hookway, 2008).

One of the key challenges evident in the use of blog and social networking profiles for research is the potential for identification of individual users' real identities. Since these sites typically provide personally identifiable information or can be aggregated to document an individual's offline identity, there is some degree of risk for researchers to use quotes or provide information in research articles as it may cause the subject personal harm. Social networking profiles may be publicly accessible and indexed via search engines, which would suggest they can be treated as open source and unprotected data from an ethical standpoint. Individuals who have set their profile to private in order to limit outsider access present an ethical dilemma as researchers must consider whether they can use such information in research. Additionally, some individuals have begun to post disclaimers on their blogs or user profiles to dissuade third parties from using their information without their expressed consent.

Email as a data source

A small number of criminologists have begun to use email as a data source for both quantitative and qualitative scholarship as the sheer quantity of email accounts and messages sent every day constitute a massive potential mine of information.

Since email is essentially a free service, researchers can readily establish and maintain accounts over long periods of time to serve as data collection points. Such techniques afford opportunities to assess the methods of scammers and fraudsters, as well as malware writers and hackers who chose to use email as an attack platform (e.g., Bohme & Holz, 2006; Frieder & Zittrain, 2007; Hanke & Hauser, 2006; Holt & Graves, 2007; King & Thomas, 2009; Nhan et al., 2009; Rege, 2009; Wall, 2004).

To date, most researchers utilise small samples of several hundred messages as a basis for analysis of mass-distribution emails, or spam, to understand the methods of scammers (e.g., Holt & Bossler, 2016). Several researchers have published studies examining advance fee fraud messages, or so-called Nigerian email scams, where the sender claims to need the help of the message recipient in order to transfer millions of dollars from one country to another (see Edelson, 2003; Holt & Graves, 2007; King & Thomas, 2009; Nhan et al., 2009). Should the recipient contact the sender to provide assistance, they will be entitled to receive a portion of the total funds. The recipient needs only provide a few hundred dollars in order to help pay attorney fees, taxes, or related costs. However, all funds sent will go to the scammer and will never lead to a good outcome for the message recipient.

Research on advance fee fraud messages illustrate that senders use one of a few different schemes, such as posing as public officials who have skimmed funds from business contracts or being a wealthy heiress with a large inheritance who needs assistance to move funds out of their country (see Edelson, 2003; Holt & Graves, 2007). The messages also include unique linguistic techniques in order to entice victims to respond, such as religious language regarding God or religious blessings, external web links to news stories to attempt to validate message claims, and emotional pleas for aid (Holt & Graves, 2007; King & Thomas, 2009; Nhan et al., 2009). Senders also tend to request potential victims provide them with their contact information, home address, phone numbers, and sometimes banking details (see Holt & Graves, 2007). In the event that a sender receives this information, they can then solicit funds from the potential recipient over time.

Kigerl's (2012, 2015, 2018) research studies of spam email provide unique examples of potential big data mining and analysis techniques for criminological inquiry. For instance, he published an analysis of the macro-level correlates of spam email distribution at the country level. The basis for this analysis was the 2008 spam archives of Untroubled Software, consisting of 725,037 messages which he coded through the use of a software script. Kigerl (2012) then extracted the originating IP address of the email and traced it to its country of origin. This data was then combined with other data sources to assess country-level economic factors and internet use variables to examine their relationship to the one-year rate of spam delivery for 132 total countries. Using regression analyses, he found that spam distribution rates were associated with a nation's gross domestic product (GDP), the number of internet users per-capita, and higher unemployment rates.

Developing metrics for hidden forms of victimisation

Though CMCs provide an immediate and obvious source of data for criminological research, there are a number of other sources that may be employed to better understand hidden forms of cybercrime. For instance, computer hacking can be examined from a fee-for-service basis when examined using forum data from underground markets. The findings limit our knowledge of the extent of victimisation, and the utility of the attacks in action. The same can be said for malicious software attacks, which are difficult to assess through traditional survey metrics as the symptoms of infection may go unrecognised by the end user (Holt & Bossler, 2016; Maimon, Kamerdze, Cukier, & Sobesto, 2013).

Enterprising researchers have found ways to assemble data sets that combine existing data sets and strategies to better understand the practices of offenders and victim targets generally. For instance, Kigerl (2013) utilised a series of data sources to triangulate the rate of piracy at the country level, combining statistics on software piracy from 1) the Business Software Alliance, 2) an analysis of the total number of active IP addresses associated with a file sharing service geolocated to a country, and 3) the number of downloads per country for four common file sharing software programs. These data provide alternative metrics to assess potential levels of file sharing and illegal downloading and served as the dependent variable to assess the macro-level economic factors affecting piracy as measured by the International Monetary Fund, the CIA World Fact Book, and the Global Competitiveness report. These measures were included in various regression models and Kigerl (2013) found that smaller, poorer countries with less technological resources had higher rates of piracy but lower piracy activity overall across all measures.

Additionally, criminologists have recently begun to use data from honeypots and Intrusion Prevention Systems (IPS) as a tool to understand the practices of computer hackers and assess the utility of deterrence theory and other frameworks to examine computer attacks. Honeypots serve as a trap tool to entice attackers and then monitor their behaviours through log file analyses (Spitzner, 2002), while IPS technologies are installed on computer networks in order to monitor network traffic, send alerts to a management server when a threat is detected, and collect information on attacks and anomalous traffic, such as its source (IP address) and level of severity (see Maimon et al., 2013 for discussion). The traffic logged by both tools is typically used by computer scientists and cybersecurity practitioners to analyse attacks and attacker behaviour, though there may be benefits to their use for criminological inquiry.

Honeypot data has gained particular attention among criminologists as they provide an opportunity to not only surreptitiously observe attacker behaviour, but also interact with intruders through various mechanisms (Jang, Kim, Song, & Park, 2013; Nasir & Al-Mousa, 2013). For example, Maimon, Alper, Sobesto, and Cukier (2014) used data from research honeypots at one major American university to test the effectiveness of warning banners as a potential deterrent to reduce the frequency and length of computer intrusions. The researchers deployed 80 honeypots on a university network and assigned each attacker to either a control group or treatment group which received a warning banner message. The warning indicated that unauthorised access was prohibited and subject to criminal and civil penalties under US laws, and that the system is being monitored and may lead to law enforcement contact.

The authors then analysed and compared the behaviours of the treatment and control group and found that 40 percent of the incidents that generated a warning banner were terminated immediately compared to only 25 percent of those incidents that did not receive a warning. This difference was not statistically significant, and banners appeared to have no impact on the frequency of repeat trespassing incidents but reduced the overall duration of the act. Thus, there may be partial utility in configuring systems to warn intruders as to their behaviours, though further study is needed to validate these claims (e.g., Holt, 2017; Maimon et al., 2013; Maimon, Wilson, Ren, & Berenblum, 2015).

The ability to implement honeypots anywhere in the globe and combine their results in a single data file presents an interesting opportunity for big data analyses of cybercrime threats (e.g., Spitzner, 2002; Maimon et al., 2015). Honeypots also have substantial limitations that directly impact their utility for social science analyses, as attacker behaviours will be unique to the environment of each honeypot limiting their generalisability across states and nations (e.g., Holt, 2017; Maimon et al., 2015). Researchers are also typically unable to distinguish the motivations of actors within any honeypot, rendering it difficult to extrapolate offenders' decision-making calculus and the factors that shape their behaviour within the environment. Thus, any use of honeypots by researchers, whether using single pots or big data collection and analysis strategies, must be careful to extend the utility or generalisability of their findings beyond their basic operational frameworks.

Challenges and dilemmas

There are a variety of different challenges and dilemmas that accompany big data research. One of the primary challenges is individual privacy online and ownership of personal content, which has led to extensive media coverage and lengthy debate (Wigan & Clarke, 2013; Williams et al., 2017). Even after excluding data that is not made publicly available for mass consumption, billions of data points are shared publicly by individual users every day, whether on social media sites, forums, or blog posts. There are also smartphone applications that automatically produce and disseminate data to third party databases, such as sleeping patterns, fitness reports, and dietary statistics on a daily basis. Although companies may give users the option to delete their data or profiles, these data are still owned and stored within their databases and records. In fact, data companies such as Google, Facebook, and Twitter use and purchase data warehouses to store all of their data and information.

It has been argued that those who organise the data describe the rights to data (Wigan & Clarke, 2013). Users are often oblivious to the fact that they voluntarily give these companies their data at virtually no cost. Furthermore, consumers may not recognise who collects their data and why it is collected, what it is used for, when it is sold to third parties, and the identity of these third parties. The details of company policies may be explained in user agreements, though most consumers neither read nor understand these documents. Thus, data rights remain with owners, while data usage agreements are defined to facilitate analysis and generation of new knowledge (Wigan & Clarke, 2013).

Another prominent issue facing big data research is obtaining adequate data samples necessary to conduct scientific inquiries (e.g., Smith et al., 2017). Since data are managed by privately owned and publicly traded firms, researchers have to obtain permission to access their data sets. Companies do not have to provide clear rationales in the event they do not provide access, making the lack of transparency and access extremely challenging. In instances where data is shared and/or sold to researchers for study purposes, data comes at an alarmingly high price (McAfee, Brynjolfsson, Davenport, Patil, & Barton, 2012). Similar to raw materials like oil, data is often valuable only after it has been processed and refined by experts in the field. Without proper coding and organisation of data, the utility of data is limited, requiring technical expertise to be handled. The costs of accessing such data may also be too exorbitant for some researchers and/ or organisations to manage.

Another challenge associated with big data research is the possibility for misinterpretations of data. Conclusions drawn from analyses of big data are only as valid as the source information whence it is generated. For instance, in 2012 and 2013, a widely cited report published in *Nature* pointed out that Google Flu Trends – a data source which calculates disease prevalence on the basis of internet searches for symptoms – highly overestimated the extent of the flu outbreak (Pentecost, 2015). In fact, people searched for flu-like symptoms without personally having been diagnosed with the disease (Pentecost, 2015). False positives developed from big data sets may be difficult to disprove due to the presumed associations with its outcomes (Wigan & Clarke, 2013). Thus, the value in big data lies not in the data itself, but in how we choose to use and operationalise it (Song et al., 2018). A failure to properly understand the strengths of big data and the patterns it identifies may lead to erroneous conclusions and findings (Wigan & Clarke, 2013).

Lastly, given the novelty of big data research, researchers may not recognise the ethical issues evident when analysing data and developing results. Researchers working with online communities that require individuals to either create an account or post in order to maintain their registration begs the question as to whether the researcher must disclose their identity to the community (see Hine, 2005; Holt, 2010; Rutter & Smith, 2005). The fact that individuals' personally identifiable information could be aggregated to document an individual's offline identity makes it difficult for researchers to use quotes and reference user content directly without increasing the risk of harm to the users. Ethics concerns like these need to be considered and handled by the research community (Silverman, 2013). Data scientists may not, however, consider these issues in advance of data collection or determine best practices to minimise risk of attribution.

Future solutions to cybercrime

With online technology, IOT data, and CMCs becoming more commonplace in society, cybercrimes that generate data loss, data manipulation, and unauthorised access to devices will increasingly require a reliable solution to mitigate their impact. As big data continues to grow in its prospects and facilities, cybercrime and cybersecurity threats will continue to emerge as urgent inquiries that need immediate solutions and long-term remedies.

There are several avenues to better manage and enforce cybercrime laws through traditional criminological mechanisms and interventions. For one, our political and legal institutions need to be better equipped to keep pace with the rapid changes in digital technology and the online landscape (Dupont, 2013). Extant research has shown that more attention and resources are needed at the government level to ensure that our law enforcement officers and government officials are up-to-date on the threats of cybercrime and cybersecurity (Bossler & Holt, 2012, 2013; Dupont, 2013; Holt & Bossler, 2012). Legislators must also find ways to better structure legal codes so that they can be more extensible to offenses that may emerge as a result of technology rather than requiring constant updates to codified law. Minimising legal loopholes and developing more effective apprehension strategies to disrupt cybercriminals in an effective manner are also essential (Dolly, 2018; Dupont, 2013).

Another possible solution to cybercrime and cybersecurity is to enhance online target hardening and digital guardianship at both the organisational and individual level. This can range from increasing the noise that hacking and malware attacks make (which allows for a faster detection process), to industries developing devices that have stricter authentication processes, as well as heavily monitored device-to-device communications (Dolly, 2018). Since data is the commodity under attack, creating strategies and methods to protect it from unauthorised access and manipulation should be a top priority for both industry and individual actors moving forward.

It is worth noting that, similar to other forms of crimes, cybercriminals are most likely to victimise entities that lack the necessary resources to defend themselves (Choi & Lee, 2017; Dolly, 2018). Targets range from industry IT systems that lack the required funds to build firm protective security platforms, to the everyday internet user who does not exercise anti-virus protection on their computer and routinely opens unidentified online attachments. Open sources with loose networks that contain great amounts of propriety data (such as educational systems) are also prime targets for cybercrime because they contain valuable information and lack the proper cybersecurity measures to safeguard itself from attacks (Dolly, 2018). In order to assuage the damage generated from cybercrimes, both public and private organisations must understand the severity of the threat posed by outdated and/or unregulated software and should conduct regular training for all of its staff and employees so that emerging cyber threats are anticipated, combatted, and ultimately mitigated.

It is evident that the rise of cybercrime presents a unique challenge for academic researchers and policy-makers, as the number of calls for service for these offenses, the composition of offender populations, and victim characteristics are not well explicated in official data sources (Brenner, 2009; Wall, 2007). Furthermore, large-scale nationally representative self-report studies of deviance and crime do not include measures for cybercriminality, making it difficult to understand the predictors and pathways to online offending (Holt & Bossler, 2016).

As a result, researchers have begun to use alternative data sources as a means to understand cybercrime. The breadth of cybercrimes that occur create data points from online sources that could be leveraged to examine these crimes. Despite the many challenges associated with big data research, it is imperative that cybercrime researchers continue to operationalise big data and data mining techniques to examine online behaviours (e.g., Benjamin et al., 2016; Holt & Bossler, 2016). Progressing in this way will not only enhance the discipline, but also improve the quality of findings in cybercrime and criminal justice sciences moving forward.

References

Andress, J., & Winterfeld, S. (2013). *Cyber warfare: Techniques, tactics and tools for security practitioners*. Waltham, MA: Elsevier.

Awan, I., & Zempi, I. (2017). "I will blow your face off": Virtual and physical world anti-muslim hate crime. *The British Journal of Criminology*, *57*(2), 362–380.

Barratt, M. J. (2012). Silk road: eBay for drugs. *Addiction*, *107*(3), 683–683.

Benjamin, V., Samtani, S., & Chen, H. (2016). Conducting large-scale analyses of underground hacker communities. In *Cybercrime through an interdisciplinary lens* (pp. 56–75). New York, NY: Taylor and Francis.

Blevins, K., & Holt, T. J. (2009). Examining the virtual subculture of johns. *Journal of Contemporary Ethnography*, *38*, 619–648.

Bocij, P. (2004). *Cyberstalking: Harassment in the Internet age and how to protect your family*. Westport, CT: Greenwood Publishing Group.

Bohme, R., & Holz, T. (2006). *The effect of stock spam on financial markets*. [Online]. Retrieved from http://ssrn.com/abstract=897431 or http://dx.doi.org/10.2139/ssrn.897431

Bossler, A. M., & Holt, T. J. (2009). On-line activities, guardianship, and malware infection: An examination of routine activities theory. *International Journal of Cyber Criminology*, *3*(1), 400–420.

Bossler, A. M., & Holt, T. J. (2012). Patrol officers' perceived role in responding to cybercrime. *Policing: An International Journal of Police Strategies & Management*, *35*(1), 165–181.

Bossler, A. M., & Holt, T. J. (2013). Assessing officer perceptions and support for online community policing. *Security Journal*, *26*(4), 349–366.

Brenner, S. W. (2009). *Cyberthreats: The emerging fault lines of the nation state*. New York, NY: Oxford University Press.

Britz, M. T. (2010). Terrorism and technology: Operationalizing cyberterrorism and identifying concepts. In *Crime on-line: Correlates, causes, and context* (pp. 193–220). Durham, NC: Carolina Academic Press.

Chan, J., & Moses, L. B. (2017). Making sense of big data for security. *British Journal of Criminology*, *57*, 299–319.

Chen, M., Mao, S., & Liu, Y. (2014). Big data: A survey. *Mobile Networks and Applications*, *19*(2), 171–209.

Choi, K. S., & Lee, J. R. (2017). Theoretical analysis of cyber-interpersonal violence victimization and offending using cyber-routine activities theory. *Computers in Human Behavior, 73,* 394–402.

Choi, K. S., Lee, S. S., & Lee, J. R. (2017). Mobile phone technology and online sexual harassment among juveniles in South Korea: Effects of self-control and social learning. *International Journal of Cyber Criminology, 11*(1), 110–127.

Clark, J. (2017, August 22). *Facing the threat: Big data and crime prevention.* [Blog post]. Retrieved from www.ibm.com/blogs/internet-of-things/big-data-crime-prevention/

Cooper, J., & Harrison, D. M. (2001). The social organization of audio piracy on the Internet. *Media, Culture, and Society, 23,* 71–89.

Cross, C. (2015). No laughing matter: Blaming the victim of online fraud. *International Review of Victimology, 21*(2), 187–204.

Cunningham, S., & Kendall, T. (2010). Sex for sale: Online commerce in the world's oldest profession. In T. J. Holt (Ed.), *Crime on-line: Correlates, causes, and context* (pp. 40–75). Raleigh, NC: Carolina Academic Press.

Decary-Hetu, D., & Dupont, B. (2012). The social network of hackers. *Global Crime, 13*(3), 160–175.

Decary-Hetu, D., & Quessy-Dore, O. (2017). Are repeat buyers in cryptomarkets loyal customers? Repeat business dyads of cryptomarket vendors and users. *American Behavioral Scientist, 61,* 1341–1357.

Dolly, J. (2018, January 9). *What does the future hold for cyber-crime?* [Blog post]. Retrieved from www.scmagazineuk.com/what-does-the-future-hold-for-cyber-crime/article/718182/

D'Ovidio, R., Mitman, T., El-Burki, I. J., & Shuman, W. (2009). Adult-child sex advocacy websites as social learning environments: A content analysis. *International Journal of Cyber Criminology, 3,* 421–440.

Dupont, B. (2013). Cybersecurity futures: How can we regulate emergent risks? *Technology Innovation Management Review, 3*(7), 6–11.

Dupont, B., Côté, A. M., Boutin, J. I., & Fernandez, J. (2017). Darkode: Recruitment patterns and transactional features of "the most dangerous cybercrime forum in the world". *American Behavioral Scientist, 61*(11), 1219–1243.

Durkin, K. F., & Bryant, C. D. (1999). Propagandizing pederasty: A thematic analysis of the online exculpatory accounts of unrepentant pedophiles. *Deviant Behavior, 20,* 103–127.

Edelson, E. (2003). The 419 scam: Information warfare on the spam front and a proposal for local filtering. *Computers and Security, 22,* 392–401.

Franklin, J., Paxson, V., Perrig, A., & Savage, S. (2007, October 29–November 2). An inquiry into the nature and cause of the wealth of internet miscreants. Paper presented at *CCS07,* Alexandria, VA.

Frederick, B. J., & Perrone, D. (2014). "Party N Play" on the Internet: Subcultural formation, craigslist, and escaping from stigma. *Deviant Behavior, 35*(11), 859–884.

Frieder, L., & Zittrain, J. (2007). Spam works: Evidence from stock touts and corresponding market activity. Berkman Center Research Publication No. 2006–11; Harvard Public Law Working Paper No. 135; Oxford Legal Studies Research Paper No. 43/2006 [Online]. Retrieved from http://ssrn.com/abstract

Furnell, S. (2002). *Cybercrime: Vandalizing the information society.* London: Addison-Wesley.

Gauthier, D. K., & Forsyth, C. J. (1999). Bareback sex, bug chasers, and the gift of death. *Deviant Behavior, 20,* 85–100.

Grov, C. (2004). Make me your death slave: Men who have sex with men and use the internet to intentionally spread HIV. *Deviant Behavior, 25*, 329–349.

GSMA. (2014). Preventing mobile payment services from being misused to monetize child sexual abuse content. *Mobile Alliance against Child Sexual Abuse Content.* [Online]. Retrieved from www.gsma.com/publicpolicy/wp-content/uploads/2016/09/GSMA2014_Report_PreventingMobilePaymentServicesFromBeingMisusedToMonetiseChildSexualAbuseContent.pdf

Hanke, M., & Hauser, F. (2006). On the effects of stock spam emails. *Journal of Financial Markets, 11*, 57–83.

Higgins, G. E., & Marcum, C. D. (2011). *Digital piracy: An integrated theoretical approach.* Raleigh, NC: Carolina Academic Press.

Hinduja, S., & Patchin, J. W. (2014). *Bullying beyond the schoolyard: Preventing and responding to cyberbullying.* Thousand Oaks, CA: Corwin Press.

Hine, C. (2005). *Virtual methods: Issues in social research on the Internet.* Oxford: Berg.

Holt, T. J. (2007). Subcultural evolution? Examining the influence of on-and off-line experiences on deviant subcultures. *Deviant Behavior, 28*(2), 171–198.

Holt, T. J. (2010). Exploring strategies for qualitative criminological and criminal justice inquiry using on-line data. *Journal of Criminal Justice Education, 21*, 300–321.

Holt, T. J. (2013a). Examining the forces shaping cybercrime markets online. *Social Science Computer Review, 31*, 165–177.

Holt, T. J. (2013b). Exploring the social organization and structure of stolen data markets. *Global Crime, 14*, 155–174.

Holt, T. J. (2017). On the value of honeypots to produce policy recommendations. *Criminology & Public Policy, 16*(3), 739–747.

Holt, T. J., & Blevins, K. R. (2007). Examining sex work from the client's perspective: Assessing johns using online data. *Deviant Behavior, 28*, 333–354.

Holt, T. J., Blevins, K. R., & Kuhns, J. B. (2008). Examining the displacement practices of johns with on-line data. *Journal of Criminal Justice, 36*(6), 522–528.

Holt, T. J., & Bossler, A. M. (2012). Predictors of patrol officer interest in cybercrime training and investigation in selected United States police departments. *Cyberpsychology, Behavior, and Social Networking, 15*(9), 464–472.

Holt, T. J., & Bossler, A. M. (2016). *Cybercrime in progress: Theory and prevention of technology-enabled offenses.* London: Routledge.

Holt, T. J., & Graves. C. (2007). A qualitative analysis of advanced feed fraud schemes. *The International Journal of Cyber Criminology, 1*, 137–154.

Holt, T. J., & Kilger, M. (2012). The social dynamics of hacking. *Know Your Enemy Series, the Honeynet Project.* [Online]. Retrieved from https://honeynet.org/papers/socialdynamics

Holt, T. J., & Lampke, E. (2010). Exploring stolen data markets on-line: Products and market forces. *Criminal Justice Studies, 23*, 33–50.

Hookway, N. (2008). Entering the blogosphere: Some strategies for using blogs in social research. *Qualitative Research, 8*, 91–113.

Horswill, A., & Weitzer, R. (2018). Becoming a client: The socialization of novice buyers of sexual services. *Deviant Behavior, 39*, 148–158.

Hutchings, A., & Holt, T. J. (2015). Crime script analysis and online black markets. *British Journal of Criminology, 55*, 596–614.

IWF. (2016). *Annual report.* [Online]. Retrieved from www.iwf.org.uk/sites/default/files/reports/2016-09/IWF%202015%20Annual%20Report%20Final%20for%20web.pdf

Jang, H., Kim, M., Song, J., & Park, H. (2013). A proactive honeynet based on feedback from a darknet. *Journal of Next Generation Information Technology, 4*(9), 69–76.

Jenkins, P. (2001). *Beyond tolerance: Child pornography on the Internet.* New York: New York University Press.

Jordan, T., & Taylor, P. (1998). A sociology of hackers. *The Sociological Review, 46,* 757–780.

Kigerl, A. C. (2012). Routine activity theory and the determinants of high cybercrime countries. *Social Science Computer Review, 30*(4), 470–486.

Kigerl, A. C. (2013). Infringing nations: Predicting software piracy rates, bittorrent tracker hosting, and p2p file sharing client downloads between countries. *International Journal of Cyber Criminology, 7*(1), 62–80.

Kigerl, A. C. (2015). Evaluation of the CAN SPAM Act: Testing deterrence and other influences of e-mail spammer legal compliance over time. *Social Science Computer Review, 33*(4), 440–458.

Kigerl, A. C. (2018). Email spam origins: Does the CAN SPAM Act shift spam beyond United States jurisdiction? *Trends in Organized Crime, 21*(1), 62–78.

King, A., & Thomas, J. (2009). You can't cheat an honest man: Making ($$$s and) sense of the Nigerian email scams. In F. Schmalleger & M. Pittaro (Eds.), *Crime of the Internet* (pp. 206–224). Saddle River, NJ: Prentice Hall.

Kosloski, A. E., Bontrager-Ryon, S., & Roe-Sepowitz, D. (2017). Buying the girl next door: A study of solicitations for sex online. *Family & Intimate Partner Violence Quarterly, 9*(4), 53–59.

Krone, T. (2004). A typology and online child pornography offending. *Trends & Issues in Crime and Criminal Justice, 279,* 2–6.

Loper, D. K. (2000). *The criminology of computer hackers: A qualitative and quantitative analysis* (Doctoral Dissertation, Michigan State University). Dissertation Abstracts International. Volume: 61–08, Section: A, page: 3362.

Maimon, D., Alper, M., Sobesto, B., & Cukier, M. (2014). Restrictive deterrent effects of a warning banner in an attacked computer system. *Criminology, 52*(1), 33–59.

Maimon, D., Kamerdze, A., Cukier, M., & Sobesto, B. (2013). Daily trends and origin of computer-focused crimes against a large university computer network. *British Journal of Criminology, 53,* 319–343.

Maimon, D., Wilson, T., Ren, W., & Berenblum, T. (2015). On the relevance of spatial and temporal dimensions in assessing computer susceptibility to system trespassing incidents. *British Journal of Criminology, 55,* 615–634.

Malesky Jr., L. A., & Ennis, L. (2004). Supportive distortions: An analysis of posts on a pedophile Internet message board. *Journal of Addictions and Offender Counseling, 24,* 92–100.

Mann, D., & Sutton, M. (1998). Netcrime: More changes in the organisation of thieving. *British Journal of Criminology, 38,* 201–229.

Maratea, R. (2011). Screwing the pooch: Legitimizing accounts in a zoophilia on-line community. *Deviant Behavior, 32*(10), 918–943.

McAfee, A., Brynjolfsson, E., Davenport, T. H., Patil, D. J., & Barton, D. (2012). Big data: The management revolution. *Harvard Business Review, 90*(10), 60–68.

Meyer, G. R. (1989). *The social organization of the computer underground.* Master's Thesis. Department of Sociology, Northern Illinois University.

Milrod, C., & Monto, M. A. (2012). The hobbyist and the girlfriend experience: Behaviors and preferences of male customers of Internet sexual service providers. *Deviant Behaviors, 33,* 792–810.

Motoyama, M., McCoy, D., Levchenko, K., Savage, S., & Voelker, G. M. (2011). An analysis of underground forums. *IMC'11*, 71–79.

Nasir, Q., & Al-Mousa, Z. A. (2013). Honeypots aiding network forensics: Challenges and notions. *JCM*, *8*(11), 700–707.

Newman, G., & Clarke, R. (2003). *Superhighway robbery: Preventing e-commerce crime*. Cullompton, NJ: Willan Press.

Nhan, J. (2013). The evolution of online piracy: Challenge and response. In T. J. Holt (Ed.), *Crime on-line: Causes, correlates, and context* (pp. 61–80). Raleigh, NC: Carolina Academic Press.

Nhan, J., Kinkade, P., & Burns, R. (2009). Finding a pot of gold at the end of an internet rainbow. *International Journal of Cyber Criminology*, *3*, 452–475.

Pentecost, M. J. (2015). Big data. *Journal of the American College of Radiology*, *12*(2), 129.

Quinn, J. F., & Forsyth, C. J. (2005). Describing sexual behavior in the era of the Internet: A typology for empirical research. *Deviant Behavior*, *26*, 191–207.

Rege, A. (2009). What's love got to do with it? Exploring online dating scams and identity fraud. *International Journal of Cyber Criminology*, *3*(2), 494–512.

Reyns, B. W., Henson, B., & Fisher, B. S. (2012). Stalking in the twilight zone: Extent of cyberstalking victimization and offending among college students. *Deviant Behavior*, *33*(1), 1–25.

Roberts, J. W., & Hunt, S. A. (2012). Social control in a sexually deviant cybercommunity: A capper's code of conduct. *Deviant Behavior*, *33*, 757–773.

Rutter, J., & Smith, G. W. (2005). Ethnographic presence in a nebulous setting. *Virtual Methods: Issues in Social Research on the Internet*, 81–92.

Schell, B. H., & Dodge, J. L. (2002). *The hacking of America: Who's doing it, why, and how*. Westport, CT: Quorum Books.

Silverman, D. (2013). *Interpreting qualitative data: Methods for analyzing talk, text, and interaction* (4nd ed.). Thousand Oaks, CA: SAGE Publications.

Smith, G. J. D., Moses, L. B., & Chan, J. (2017). The challenges of doing criminology in the Big Data era: Towards a digital and data-driven approach. *British Journal of Criminology*, *57*, 259–274.

Song, J., Song, T. M., & Lee, J. R. (2018). Stay alert: Forecasting the risks of sexting in Korea using social big data. *Computers in Human Behavior*, *81*, 294–302.

Song, T. M., Song, J., An, J. Y., Hayman, L. L., & Woo, J. M. (2014). Psychological and social factors affecting Internet searches on suicide in Korea: A big data analysis of Google search trends. *Yonsei Medical Journal*, *55*(1), 254–263.

Spitzner, L. (2002). *Honeypots: Tracking hackers*. Boston: MA: Addison-Wesley Longman.

Symantec Corporation. (2013). *Symantec Internet security threat report* (Vol. 18). [Online]. Retrieved from www.symantec.com/threatreport/

Tewksbury, R. (2003). Bareback sex and the quest for HIV: Assessing the relationship in Internet personal advertisements of men who have sex with men. *Deviant Behavior*, *24*, 467–482.

Tewksbury, R. (2006). "Click here for HIV": An analysis of internet-based bug chasers and bug givers. *Deviant Behavior*, *27*, 379–395.

Wall, D. S. (2001). Cybercrimes and the Internet. In D. S. Wall (Ed.), *Crime and the Internet* (pp. 1–17). New York: Routledge.

Wall, D. S. (2004). Digital realism and the governance of spam as cybercrime. *European Journal on Criminal Policy and Research*, *10*, 309–335.

Wall, D. S. (2007). *Cybercrime: The transformation of crime in the information age* (Vol. 4). Malden, MA: Polity Press.

Weimann, G. (2005). How modern terrorism uses the Internet. *The Journal of International Security Affairs, 8.*

Wigan, M. R., & Clarke, R. (2013). Big Data's big unintended consequences. *Computer, 46*(6), 46–53.

Williams, J. P., & Copes, H. (2005). "How edge are you?" Constructing authentic identities and subcultural boundaries in a straightedge internet forum. *Symbolic Interaction, 28*(1), 67–89.

Williams, M. L., Burnap, P., & Sloan, L. (2017). Crime sensing with Big Data: The affordances and limitations of using open-source communications to estimate crime patterns. *British Journal of Criminology, 57*, 320–340.

Wu, X., Zhu, X., Wu, G. Q., & Ding, W. (2014). Data mining with big data. *IEEE Transactions on Knowledge and Data Engineering, 26*(1), 97–107.

Yar, M. (2013). *Cybercrime and Society* (2nd ed.). London: SAGE Publications.

Yip, M., Webber, C., & Shadbolt, N. (2013). Trust among cybercriminals? Carding forums, uncertainty, and implications for policing. *Policing and Society, 23*, 1–24.

7 Genetics, bioethics, and big data

Melissa J. Green

Genetic variation likely contributes to individual difference in complex human traits – such as stress-response physiology and personality features including impulsivity and risk taking – that influence the manifestation of antisocial and aggressive behaviours, or criminal offending (Kreek, Nielsen, Butelman, & LaForge, 2005). While a bulk of evidence suggests that common polymorphisms regulating monoamine, dopamine, and serotonergic systems play some role in contributing to aggressive behaviour, their neurobiological mechanisms are unclear, and there remains much to understand about the likely moderating effects of a range of environmental exposures, as implicated in a number of recent studies (Barnes & Jacobs, 2013; Brennan et al., 2011; Lu & Menard, 2017; Tuvblad et al., 2016; Wagner et al., 2010; Zhang, Cao, Wang, Ji, & Cao, 2016). For example, a recent meta-analysis of 27 studies testing the interaction of the monoamine oxidase A [*MAOA*] genotype and childhood adversities on antisocial outcomes in *non-clinical samples* (Byrd & Manuck, 2014) suggests that genetic variants traditionally regarded as 'risk' variants might be better regarded conferring *sensitivity to environmental influences* (see also Belsky et al., 2009). In the case of *MAOA*, accumulating findings suggest that one genetic variant of this polymorphism confers susceptibility to the negative influence of adverse environmental exposures such as childhood maltreatment, while the other variant may confer resilience under conditions of positive environmental exposures (Caspi et al., 2002; Iofrida, Palumbo, & Pellegrini, 2014; Zhang et al., 2016). While the earliest molecular genetic studies focused on candidate genes with known effects on neurotransmitter systems that should theoretically impact these traits and behaviours (Iofrida et al., 2014), more recent efforts have employed large-scale genome-wide associations studies that have failed to implicate these candidate genes (likely due to rigorous thresholds for statistical significance) (Rautiainen et al., 2016; Tielbeek et al., 2017; Tielbeek et al., 2012). Alarmingly, the genetic risk factors associated with impulsive aggression and criminal behaviours have recently impacted the decisions of a jury in Italy (Forzano et al., 2010), where sentences have been reduced in light of the defendant being said to have a genetic predisposition to impulsive behaviours under stressful circumstances, thereby mitigating the perception of responsibility, but also reinforcing ideas of genetic determinism (Baum, 2011). These are potentially dangerous precedents in an era where biobanking of genetic and other information allows unprecedented access to individual genomic profiles with the potential for them to be brought to bear on myriad criminal proceedings. In this chapter, a discussion of the emerging bioethical issues in the context of modern large-scale biobanking initiatives is presented, in an era when comprehensive understanding of the meaning of genetic 'risk' for antisocial behaviour is arguably more slender than the use of large-scale genomic data in this field can currently justify.

Genetic testimony in judicial systems

While certain genes and neurobiological processes may predispose some people to aggressive or violent behaviour, there are serious limitations in our understanding of the way that these risk factors contribute to human behaviour. With increasing yet still not complete knowledge of these mechanisms, defendants are increasingly likely to introduce genetic evidence of an inherited disposition to be considered in an attempt to avoid moral culpability for a crime: whether such evidence may be used to determine legal liability when evaluating whether a defendant is less morally culpable, or less deserving of punishment, has been the topic of recent debate (Segal, 2016). In particular, the genetic research mentioned earlier raises the question of whether testimony regarding a defendant's genotype, exposure to adverse environments during childhood (such as domestic violence or maltreatment) and/or the experience of high levels of stress is appropriate to present during the proceedings of criminal trials, especially when capital punishment is a consideration (Bernet, Vnencak-Jones, Farahany, & Montgomery, 2007). Discussion of these issues by Baum (2011) and Iofrida et al. (2014) provides several examples of the presentation of genetic evidence in courts in France, Italy, and the US, in which consideration of behavioural genetics has been considered with different outcomes over the past 70 years; only recently has the presentation of genetic evidence resulted in a reduced penalty applied to a defendant, on account of the predisposition being judged to mitigate moral responsibility.

As discussed by Forzano et al. (2010), a violent stabbing murder case in Italy was the first to present a comprehensive genetic and biological profile in defence of the crime, together with the other evidence including psychiatric and cognitive assessments, and structural and functional brain imaging scans (notably, the defendant was diagnosed with schizophrenia). The inclusion of these assessments alongside the genetic profile of the defendant resulted in the reduction of the prison sentence by one year (from nine to eight years), largely because he was a carrier of several genetic variants thought to be associated with a predisposition to violence and impulsivity. The judge based his sentence on these indicators of the accused being affected by a mental disorder, such that he was not fully capable of understanding the seriousness of his actions and was particularly prone to be aggressive under stressful circumstances (Forzano et al., 2010). Forzano discusses the risks of offering susceptibility testing in the context of legal proceedings despite the lack of clear evidence of the clinical utility of these genetic variants (Fox, 1971).

There have been several other cases in which the presentation of biological evidence from genetics and neuroimaging influenced the outcome of criminal proceedings in the form of a decision of diminished responsibility. The earliest genetic evidence presented in a criminal murder case in France (*Hugon*, 1968) was in relation to the homicide of an elderly prostitute in Paris; the defendant carried an additional Y chromosome (a condition known as XYY syndrome), and had a reputation for aggression that was argued to be an innate predisposition to crime on account of this extra Y chromosome. Despite very limited scientific evidence for this link, the permission of evidence resulted in mitigation of his sentence (Fox, 1971). Seven years later, in the US (Yukl, 1975), submission of evidence to the jury for the same XYY condition, in relation to the murder of a 23-year-old woman, was deemed unreliable. While the judge agreed to the insanity defence, the jurors rejected it; both the legal and the scientific community agreed that the association between this chromosomal condition and violent behaviour was not reliable (Iofrida et al., 2014).

In another case in the US (*Mobley*, 1994), the defence lawyer asked that the defendant be tested for the *MAOA* 'risk' genotype as a mitigating factor, but the court declined the request even though there was indisputable evidence of a family history of violence; in this case, the defendant was executed (Iofrida et al., 2014). Two other cases in Italy have resulted in either case acquittal or reduced sentencing. In the first, reported in 2010 (Rigoni et al., 2010), a woman was convicted for killing her newborn child immediately after birth; she carried five genetic variants which have been previously associated with violence and impulsivity, and a structural brain scan revealed reduced grey matter volume in the left prefrontal cortex, known to be involved in cognitive and behavioural inhibition. The defendant also had a history of alcohol and polydrug abuse, and expert evaluation concluded that her high impulsivity and aggressive tendencies were consistent with borderline personality disorder. However, the experts' testimony was not included in the sentencing because the case was acquitted due to lack of evidence (Iofrida et al., 2014). In the second case, tried in a court in Como (*Albertani*, 2011), a woman was convicted for the murder of her sister and attempted murder of her mother; the testimony included presentation of the defendant's genetic variation and structural brain changes said to be associated with violence and impulsivity, and resulted in the prison sentence being reduced from 30 years to 20 years, preceded by a period of at least three years in a mental hospital for a therapeutic and rehabilitation program. In one other case in the US (*Waldroup*, 2011), a man charged with the brutal murder of his wife's friend and attempted murder of his wife was given a prison sentence reduced to 32 years instead of the death penalty on the basis of genetic information and a history of severe child abuse (Baum, 2011).

The genetics of criminal behaviour clearly has the potential to make a considerable impact on society and the law. Notably, the decisions to mitigate sentences for violent crimes such as those described earlier rests on the assumption that these criminal acts represent 'instinctive' reactions to provocations committed, driven by impulsive violence rather than premeditated actions (Iofrida et al., 2014). As noted by Forzano et al. (2010), the implications of any biological predisposition toward impulsive aggression or antisocial criminal behaviour has the potential to set a precedent that wrongly assumes biological determinism, which may unduly influence judicial enquiry and sentencing in the future. However, as noted previously, the genes associated with aggressive and violent behaviours in humans appear not to represent deterministic 'risk' genes, but instead operate via differential susceptibility to both negative and positive environmental exposures that may increase or decrease risk to aggression and/or criminal behaviours. Without due acknowledgement of this complexity, the increasing availability of biobanking initiatives with genomic data linked to other biological and social information related to the individual (e.g., criminal offending records, psychiatric diagnoses) that are fast becoming commonplace have the potential to be misused in this context without appropriate safeguards and education of experts working in the criminal justice system.

The ethical and legal implications of the mass storage and access to genetic material within population biobanking and data-sharing networks around the world presents very complex issues that are discussed in the next sections.

Genetics and bioethics in the age of big data

With rapid advances in genomics and information technology, both governments and industry have recently invested in organised collections of population-based health data and biological samples (Swede, Stone, & Norwood, 2007) for the purpose of innovation and discovery in biomedical research and improvements in human health (Dove, Laurie, & Knoppers, 2017; Gulcher, Kong, & Stefansson, 2001; Wang et al., 2017). The most comprehensive type of population-based biobank is designed to link biological tissue (e.g., DNA, or other molecular markers derived from blood, saliva, urine, or diseased tissue) with medical history and lifestyle information, such as routinely collected information in an individual's medical records or other government (administrative) databases. Highly publicised examples include the UK Biobank (Sudlow et al., 2015), the US Precision Medicine Initiative (NIH, 2016), and Human Genome Projects (Lander, Linton, Birren, & Consortium, 2001), while at least 10 other countries have established national biobanks, including in Canada (Awadalla et al., 2013), Norway (Skolbekken, Ursin, Solberg, Christensen, & Ytterhus, 2005), the Netherlands (Boeckhout & Douglas, 2015), Germany (Hirschberg, Knuppel, & Strech, 2013), South Africa (Rheeder, 2017), Singapore (Waldby, 2009), Iceland, Estonia, Latvia, Japan, Sweden, and the Kingdom of Tonga (Austin, Harding, & McElroy, 2003; Swede et al., 2007). Interestingly, public opposition saw the closing of the biobank in the Kingdom of Tonga, and privacy protection surrounding the Icelandic (deCODE) initiative (Gulcher et al., 2001) was ruled unconstitutional in 2003. Despite being the world's first population-wide genomic biobank, the Icelandic biobank has since been decommissioned, highlighting the profound ethical and legal challenges that such large scale biobanking poses to governments and participating individuals. While the vast majority of these population-based biobanks were established with the informed consent of the individuals whose biological material is contained in them, ethical and legal issues concerning consent and protection of privacy, and ownership and control over the use of biobank data continue to be debated (Caulfield & Murdoch, 2017; Dhai, Mahomed, & Sanne, 2015; Dove et al., 2017; Miller & Tucker, 2017; Vayena, Salathe, Madoff, & Brownstein, 2015). These bioethical issues are increasingly important given growing interest in the use of 'residual' specimens (i.e., leftover tissue) acquired in the context of a specific research investigation or after clinical procedures in hospitals, for which informed consent may not have been obtained at the time of their collection for clinical or specific research purposes (Cunningham, O'Doherty, Senecal, Secko, & Avard, 2015). Of particular concern in both instances is the reporting of incidental clinically actionable findings to participants who may have opted to remain anonymous during consent processes (Wallace & Kent, 2011; Wolf et al., 2012).

Pertinent to these ongoing bioethical debates, is the need for government, industry, and multiple researchers to be involved in the administration and use of biobanked data, given the long-term nature of biobanking initiatives and the impracticality of obtaining informed consent for each and every use of a participating individual's tissue or health data. For example, it is impossible to predict all future research questions that an end-user (academic or industry partner) might ask of biobanked data to enable a participant to feasibly consent to all potential uses of their specimens (Caulfield et al., 2008). As such, broad or 'open consent' strategies that deviate from traditional legal norms have been adopted by the majority of population-wide biobanking initiatives, with questions remaining about their legal and ethical appropriateness (Caulfield, 2015; Edwards, Cadigan, Evans, & Henderson, 2014; Eriksson & Helgesson, 2005). Other options for 'dynamic consent' have been put forward (Kaye et al., 2015), especially in relation to the use of personal data by third parties. Ongoing efforts to resolve these issues include new data protection legislation developed by the European Union (EU, 2016; Hallinan & Friedewald, 2015; Hallinan, Friedewald, & De Hert, 2013) that was applied from May 2018; at this time, the General Data Protection Regulation (GDPR) came into effect, providing a regulatory framework in response to privacy concerns that relate to biobanks, but also broader concerns arising from an ever-expanding market of digitised consumer and mobile technologies (Rumbold & Pierscionek, 2017). The new regulation serves to protect individuals' rights to privacy and other freedoms, while simultaneously facilitating the exchange of data as required for the common good; the policy has specific clauses relating to the processing of genetic and health data, and personal data relating to criminal convictions and offences. In particular, 'broad consent' for scientific research will be permissible according to recognised ethical standards. However, this does not equate to 'blanket' or 'open' consent in the case of biobanking research for which the perceived risks are minimal when weighed against the potential benefits (Sheehan, 2011). While the GDPR makes some effort to address issues for biomedical research when consent has not been explicitly obtained from the individual (e.g., use of residual data) – noting that this may be possible when such research conforms to the public's best interest – key issues remain unresolved, such as the definition of 'public interest' or 'pressing social need' (Rumbold &

Pierscionek, 2017). One significant issue for current practices is that, according to the new GDPR legislation, pseudonymised data will be treated as personal data (where personal data is defined as that which can identify an individual). Pseudonymised data – for example, where identifiers are removed and replaced with a unique code that can be traced back to the (re-identified) individual – was previously regarded as sufficient to protect privacy. However, truly anonymised data would not be able to be traced back to the person's identity. Pseudonymised data is thus recognised as allowing incidental findings to be traced back to the (re-identified) individual, and/or their contributed biological or health data to be verified, and the new change in legislation has resulted from acknowledgement of vulnerability (potential identification of individuals) when pseudonymised data are used, compared to the protection afforded by true anonymisation (Rumbold & Pierscionek, 2017).

Big data and biobanking in the criminology context

The repurposing of genetic data without consent or knowledge of the individual, for use in perpetuity, raises ethical and legal questions about data ownership and consent processes, as discussed earlier in relation to health biobanks. These ethical debates are just as pertinent to public participation in forensic DNA databases (Tutton & Levitt, 2010). While medical research biobanks are seen to facilitate innovation in public health, with participation typically voluntary and based on individual rights and choices, forensic DNA databases involve the collection, storage, and use of DNA profiles from suspects, convicted offenders, victims, volunteers, and other persons of interest to criminal investigation work, so that the profiles can be compared with those obtained from crime scene samples to facilitate crime investigations and suspect identification. Thus, forensic DNA 'banks' are primarily used for law enforcement purposes, yet do not employ the same processes of consent or privacy protection regarding the use of personal and biological data (Machado & Silva, 2015). Extreme examples of disregard for the re-use of existing biological specimens for these purposes include the Texas Department of State Health Services releasing 800 DNA samples to the US Armed Forces DNA Identification Laboratory for creation of a forensic database. In addition, in 2003, the assassination of a Swedish politician led to police requesting access to the suspect's DNA from a national Newborn Screening biobank to compare to DNA extracted from the crime scene; the police were granted access by the biobank without court involvement, and a conviction later resulted (O'Doherty et al., 2016).

More recently, detectives the US state of California used a public genealogy database to identify a suspect in the 'Golden State Killer' cases, for which investigations had gone cold decades ago. In this instance, the police had a well-preserved sample of their prime suspect's DNA from one of the crime scenes (who had been linked to more than 50 rapes and 12 murders from 1976 to 1986) but no means of identifying the individual whose DNA they had in their possession. In a new twist on the use of stored DNA for forensic investigations, the detectives uploaded the suspect's DNA sample into a public database (which likely would have asked them to certify that the DNA was their own or belonged to someone for whom they were legal guardians, or that they had obtained authorisation for upload) and bingo! A DNA match was found with a relative who had taken part in personal genomic testing, giving the detectives the lead that they needed to locate the identity of the killer. These events have thus reignited debate about genetic privacy, given that many members of the general public engage in these genetic testing activities online for the purpose of finding out information about their genealogy, but not with the intent of compromising their family for generations to come. A fundamental question of ethics is raised for which there are no easy answers.

Curiously, the governance of forensic DNA databases and health biobanks have generally been treated as separate fields of debate and analysis with regard to the complex ethical issues surrounding their use for law enforcement by primary or other parties. This is often justified on the basis of the purpose of forensic DNA databases compared to that of biomedical data stored in population-based biobanks, but there are reasons to question this dogma. Why should crime prevention be morally favoured over disease prevention? It has indeed been argued by others (Machado & Silva, 2015) that issues of civil rights, the right to privacy, data integrity, and the presumption of innocence should be considered in relation to the use of forensic DNA, even when the purpose is crime detection and prevention. This may be especially pertinent in relation to retention of samples and profiles of individuals who are not subsequently brought before the courts or in cases where guilt is not established.

Around the world, forensic DNA databases operate to achieve success in criminal law enforcement. In the UK, a DNA (forensic) database was first established in 1995 for routine use in the investigation of crime. Notably, establishment of this National DNA Database (NDNAD) was undertaken with the assumption that these processes would not infringe any civil rights issues as initially these results are not assigned to any individual, and their use in the criminal justice system was perceived as an essential 'social good' (Martin, 2004). Conversely, the UK biobank had its legitimacy questioned from the outset due to the nature and historical stigma associated with collecting large data sets from individuals that are then used in open-ended research in perpetuity (Tutton & Levitt, 2010). While the NDNAD's initial charter was to collect and house samples from criminals, this objective expanded over time, with UK legislation changing the size and scope of the database, largely as an attempt to combat youth antisocial behaviour. Thus, within the UK NDNAD, samples can be taken without consent and stored for life from those over the age of 10 years, and there is no right to withdraw samples by those arrested and convicted of any type of offence, or even from those acquitted or mistakenly arrested. For the victims of crime there is a requirement for consent but ultimately limited scope for withdrawal of samples. While the NDNAD maintains that innocent individuals with genetic profiles stored in these databases have nothing to fear, it has been the stance of many legal, ethical, and advocacy groups to disagree and assert that this state-imposed determination is a threat to civil rights and in particular for certain individuals or groups. For example, retention of samples from arrestees for relatively small offences may be significant in relation to minority ethnic groups, with potentially harmful ethnic and social consequences (Williams & Wienroth, 2014). The majority of European countries now have either operational NDNADs, although there is diversity in the operation of the various NDNADs with regard to the laws allowing profiles to be obtained and retained from individuals who are either suspected or convicted of crimes, and for the use of samples for profiling. For example, in England, Austria, Finland, Denmark, Hungary, Slovenia, and Croatia, any obtained samples can be retained for future testing, while in the other countries, samples must be destroyed after the profile is obtained or once a court has reached a decision (Martin, 2004). Notably, the success of some European NDNADs can be attributed to the retention of personal DNA profiles indefinitely. NDNADs in France do not compel the donation of DNA by all suspects, and legislation allows requests for removal of DNA; in the US, DNA is only required from individuals convicted of certain types of offences, and there are federal and state laws to mitigate unauthorised use of any stored information (Martin, 2004).

Undoubtedly, the success of NDNADs means that there is unlikely to be a significant change in their use, regardless of the ethical issues that they raise in parallel with biomedical biobanking. However, some claim that there is a compelling need for proactive public discussion of the benefits and risks

> in a context in which biobanks and forensic DNA databases are seen as social assets that must make their conduct explicit to the participants on the basis of community values and the social, political and ethical consequences of medical research or criminal investigation.
>
> (Machado & Silva, 2015, p. 823)

Key questions for clarification include the rights of ownership of personal data, the unequal distribution of risks and benefits among certain ethic and minority populations, conflicts of interests between public and private entities, and between research, industry, and business interests in criminal investigation (Machado & Silva, 2014). These issues have certainly plagued biobanks for use in medical research, for which active consent to contribute biological data is the normative model for ethical participation.

The future of big data and genetics in criminology

The increased accessibility and interest in using genetic information for research and criminal proceedings is occurring at an exponential rate. However, given that the utility of genetic profiling for the purpose of establishing the extent of 'inherited' risk for impulsive aggression and antisocial criminal behaviour lacks robust scientific evidence, the question of whether this should mitigate moral or legal liability *even if scientifically supported* remains open for future debate. There is a danger that any (even partial) attribution of biological causes to criminal acts will be misinterpreted as reductionist determinism, and such simplistic causal relationships between genetic variants and aggressive or violent behaviour must be avoided.

In parallel, ethical and legal debates about the legitimacy of long term storage of forensic DNA data in what are essentially biobanks by another name raise questions about the social value placed upon the use of such data for biomedical research versus criminal proceedings. When established *without* the informed consent of the individuals whose biological material is contained in them (as is the case with many forensic DNA databanks), there are potentially higher stakes in terms of the ethical and legal issues concerning consent and protection of privacy, and ownership and control of data that deserve explicit public and expert debate with the level of consideration that medical research practices are subjected to. This will call on the need for ethicists, lawyers, and minorities who are likely to be disproportionately affected to come together and discus the potential unintended consequences of genetic data if used for purposes other than that for which it was collected.

Ethical guidelines for the use of personal (biological) data obtained with or without the consent of the individual must obviously focus on the weight the potential social benefit against any harm to an individual whose data might be used (with or without their knowledge) for progress in health care or criminal justice. Consideration of the definition of these terms must allow them to be fluid in different contexts (e.g., when impacting on disadvantaged minorities). Relevant legislation and ethical guidelines relating to the secondary use of stored genetic material for both research and industry is taking place globally in an effort to bring policy up to speed with the capacity for genomic testing and data availability in the current era. However, issues of personal liberty (i.e., ownership of biological data) versus public good seem relatively less controversial to navigate in a biomedical context – requiring public education campaigns and an understanding of the utility of population genomics to make a difference to health care – than do the same issues for use mass genomic data by industry or criminal justice systems. The latter bring forth serious issues such as inequality and conflict of interest (e.g., in terms of potential exploitation by business) that must be considered an open and public debate of their social values to ensure that civil rights are respected in this era of big data and genomics.

References

Austin, M. A., Harding, S., & McElroy, C. (2003). Genebanks: A comparison of eight proposed international genetic databases. *Journal of Community Genetics, 6*(1), 37–45. doi:10.1159/000069544

Awadalla, P., Boileau, C., Payette, Y., Idaghdour, Y., Goulet, J. P., Knoppers, N., . . . Project, C. A. (2013). Cohort profile of the CARTaGENE study: Quebec's population-based biobank for public health and personalized genomics. *International Journal of Epidemiology, 42*(5), 1285–1299.

Barnes, J. C., & Jacobs, B. A. (2013). Genetic risk for violent behavior and environmental exposure to disadvantage and violent crime: The case for gene-environment interaction. *Journal of Interpersonal Violence, 28*(1), 92–120. doi:10.1177/0886260512448847

Baum, M. L. (2011). The Monoamine Oxidase A (MAOA) genetic predisposition to impulsive violence: Is it relevant to criminal trials? *Neuroethics, 6*(2), 287–306. doi:10.1007/s12152-011-9108-6

Belsky, J., Jonassaint, C., Pluess, M., Stanton, M., Brummett, B., & Williams, R. (2009). Vulnerability genes or plasticity genes? *Molecular Psychiatry, 14*(8), 746–754. https://dx.doi.org/10.1038/mp.2009.44

Bernet, W., Vnencak-Jones, C. L., Farahany, N., & Montgomery, S. A. (2007). Bad nature, bad nurture, and testimony regarding MAOA and SLC6A4 genotyping at murder trials. *Journal of Forensic Sciences, 52*(6), 1362–1371. doi:10.1111/j.1556-4029.2007.00562.x

Boeckhout, M., & Douglas, C. M. (2015). Governing the research-care divide in clinical biobanking: Dutch perspectives. *Life Sciences, Society and Policy, 11*(7). doi:10.1186/s40504-015-0025-z

Brennan, P. A., Hammen, C., Sylvers, P., Bor, W., Najman, J., Lind, P., . . . Smith, A. K. (2011). Interactions between the COMT Val108/158Met polymorphism and maternal prenatal smoking predict aggressive behavior outcomes. *Biological Psychology, 87*(1), 99–105. https://dx.doi.org/10.1016/j.biopsycho.2011.02.013

Byrd, A. L., & Manuck, S. B. (2014). MAOA, childhood maltreatment, and antisocial behavior: Meta-analysis of a gene-environment interaction. *Biological Psychiatry, 75*(1), 9–17. doi:10.1016/j.biopsych.2013.05.004

Caspi, A., McClay, J., Moffitt, T. E., Mill, J., Martin, J., Craig, I. W., . . . Poulton, R. (2002). Role of genotype in the cycle of violence in maltreated children. *Science, 297*(5582), 851–854.

Caulfield, T. (2015). Biobanks and blanket consent: The proper place of the public good and public perception rationales. *King's Law Journal, 18*(2), 209–226. doi:10.1080/09615768.2007.11427674

Caulfield, T., McGuire, A. L., Cho, M., Buchanan, J. A., Burgess, M. M., Danilczyk, U., . . . Timmons, M. (2008). Research ethics recommendations for whole-genome research: Consensus statement. *PLoS Biology, 6*(3), e73. doi:10.1371/journal.pbio.0060073

Caulfield, T., & Murdoch, B. (2017). Genes, cells, and biobanks: Yes, there's still a consent problem. *PLoS Biology, 15*(7), e2002654. doi:10.1371/journal.pbio.2002654

Cunningham, S., O'Doherty, K. C., Senecal, K., Secko, D., & Avard, D. (2015). Public concerns regarding the storage and secondary uses of residual newborn bloodspots: An analysis of print media, legal cases, and public engagement activities. *Journal of Community Genetics, 6*(2), 117–128. doi:10.1007/s12687-014-0206-0

Dhai, A., Mahomed, S., & Sanne, I. (2015). Biobanks and human health research: Balancing progress and protections. *South African Journal of Bioethics and Law, 8*(2), 55. doi:10.7196/sajbl.8060

Dove, E. S., Laurie, G. T., & Knoppers, B. M. (2017). Data sharing and privacy. In G.S. Ginsburg and H.F. Willard, *Genomic and Precision Medicine: Foundatioons, Translation, and Implementation,* 143–160. New York, NY: Elsevier. doi:10.1016/b978-0-12-800681-8.00010-4

Edwards, T., Cadigan, R. J., Evans, J. P., & Henderson, G. E. (2014). Biobanks containing clinical specimens: Defining characteristics, policies, and practices. *Clinical Biochemistry, 47*(4–5), 245–251. doi:10.1016/j.clinbiochem.2013.11.023

Eriksson, S., & Helgesson, G. (2005). Potential harms, anonymization, and the right to withdraw consent to biobank research. *European Journal of Human Genetics, 13*(9), 1071–1076. doi:10.1038/sj.ejhg.5201458

EU. (2016). *General data protection regulation 2016/679.* Retrieved from http://eur-lex.europa.eu/eli/reg/2016/679/oj

Forzano, F., Borry, P., Cambon-Thomsen, A., Hodgson, S. V., Tibben, A., de Vries, P., . . . Cornel, M. (2010). Italian appeal court: A genetic predisposition to commit murder? *Eur Journal of Human Genetics, 18*(5), 519–521. doi:10.1038/ejhg.2010.31

Fox, R. G. (1971). The XYY offender: A modern myth? *Journal of Criminal Law, Criminology and Police Science, 62,* 59–73.

Gulcher, J. R., Kong, A., & Stefansson, K. (2001). The role of linkage studies for common diseases. *Current Opinion in Genetics Development, 11,* 264–267.

Hallinan, D., & Friedewald, M. (2015). Open consent, biobanking and data protection law: Can open consent be "informed" under the forthcoming data protection regulation? *Life Sciences, Society and Policy, 11*(1). doi:10.1186/s40504-014-0020-9

Hallinan, D., Friedewald, M., & De Hert, P. (2013). Genetic data and the data protection regulation: Anonymity, multiple subjects, sensitivity and a prohibitionary logic regarding genetic data? *Computer Law & Security Review, 29*(4), 317–329. doi:10.1016/j.clsr.2013.05.013

Hirschberg, I., Knuppel, H., & Strech, D. (2013). Practice variation across consent templates for biobank research: A survey of German biobanks. *Frontiers in Genetics, 4*(240). doi:10.3389/fgene.2013.00240

Iofrida, C., Palumbo, S., & Pellegrini, S. (2014). Molecular genetics and antisocial behavior: Where do we stand? *Experimental Biology and Medicine (Maywood), 239*(11), 1514–1523. doi:10.1177/1535370214529508

Kaye, J., Whitley, E. A., Lund, D., Morrison, M., Teare, H., & Melham, K. (2015). Dynamic consent: A patient interface for twenty-first century research networks. *European Journal of Human Genetics, 23*(2), 141–146. doi:10.1038/ejhg.2014.71

Kreek, M. J., Nielsen, D. A., Butelman, E. R., & LaForge, K. S. (2005). Genetic influences on impulsivity, risk taking, stress responsivity and vulnerability to drug abuse and addiction. *Nature Neuroscience, 8*(11), 1450–1457. doi:10.1038/nn1583

Lander, E. S., Linton, L. M., Birren, B., & Consortium, a. t. I. H. G. M. (2001). Initial sequencing and analysis of the human genome. *Nature, 409,* 860–921.

Lu, Y. F., & Menard, S. (2017). The interplay of MAOA and peer influences in predicting adult criminal behavior. *Psychiatric Quarterly, 88*(1), 115–128. doi:10.1007/s11126-016-9441-3

Machado, H., & Silva, S. (2014). "Would you accept having your DNA profile inserted in the National Forensic DNA database? Why?" Results of a questionnaire applied in Portugal. *Forensic Science International Genetics, 8*(1), 132–136. doi:10.1016/j.fsigen.2013.08.014

Machado, H., & Silva, S. (2015). Public participation in genetic databases: Crossing the boundaries between biobanks and forensic DNA databases through the principle of solidarity. *Journal of Medical Ethics, 41*(10), 820–824. doi:10.1136/medethics-2014-102126

Martin, P. D. (2004). National DNA databases: Practice and practicability: A forum for discussion. *International Congress Series, 1261,* 1–8. doi:10.1016/s0531-5131(03)01844-2

Miller, A. R., & Tucker, C. (2017). Privacy protection, personalized medicine, and genetic testing. *Management Science.* doi:10.1287/mnsc.2017.2858

NIH. (2016). *National Institutes of Health funds biobank to support Precision Medicine Initiative cohort program.* U.S. Department of Health and Human Services. Retrieved from https://www.nih.gov/news-events/news-releases/nih-funds-biobank-support-precision-medicine-initiative-cohort-program

O'Doherty, K. C., Christofides, E., Yen, J., Bentzen, H. B., Burke, W., Hallowell, N., . . . Willison, D. J. (2016). If you build it, they will come: Unintended future uses of organised health data collections. *BMC Medical Ethics, 17*(1), 54. doi:10.1186/s12910-016-0137-x

Rautiainen, M. R., Paunio, T., Repo-Tiihonen, E., Virkkunen, M., Ollila, H. M., Sulkava, S., . . . Tiihonen, J. (2016). Genome-wide association study of antisocial personality disorder. *Translational Psychiatry, 6*(9), e883. doi:10.1038/tp.2016.155

Rheeder, R. (2017). Biobanks in South Africa: A global perspective on privacy and confidentiality. *South African Medical Journal, 107*(5), 390–393. doi:10.7196/SAMJ.2017. v107i5.12004

Rigoni, D., Pellegrini, S., Mariotti, V., Cozza, A., Mechelli, A., Ferrara, S. D., . . . Sartori, G. (2010). How neuroscience and behavioral genetics improve psychiatric assessment: Report on a violent murder case. *Frontiers in Behavioural Neuroscience, 4*, 160.

Rumbold, J. M., & Pierscionek, B. (2017). The effect of the general data protection regulation on medical research. *Journal of Medical Internet Research, 19*(2), e47. doi:10.2196/jmir.7108

Segal, J. B. (2016). Inherited proclivity: When should neurogenetics mitigate moral culpability for purposes of sentencing? *Journal of Law and the Biosciences, 3*(1), 227–237. doi:10.1093/jlb/lsw005

Sheehan, M. (2011). Can broad consent be informed consent? *Public Health Ethics, 4*(3), 226–235. doi:10.1093/phe/phr020

Skolbekken, J.-A., Ursin, L. Ø., Solberg, B., Christensen, E., & Ytterhus, B. (2005). Not worth the paper it's written on? Informed consent and biobank research in a Norwegian context. *Critical Public Health, 15*(4), 335–347. doi:10.1080/09581590500523319

Sudlow, C., Gallacher, J., Allen, N., Beral, V., Burton, P., Danesh, J., . . . Collins, R. (2015). UK biobank: An open access resource for identifying the causes of a wide range of complex diseases of middle and old age. *PLoS Medicine, 12*(3), e1001779. doi:10.1371/journal.pmed.1001779

Swede, H., Stone, C. L., & Norwood, A. R. (2007). National population-based biobanks for genetic research. *Genetics in Medicine, 9*(3), 141–149. doi:10.1097/GIM.0b013e3180 330039

Tielbeek, J. J., Johansson, A., Polderman, T. J. C., Rautiainen, M. R., Jansen, P., Taylor, M., . . . Broad Antisocial Behavior Consortium, c. (2017). Genome-wide association studies of a broad spectrum of antisocial behavior. *JAMA Psychiatry, 74*(12), 1242–1250. https://dx.doi.org/10.1001/jamapsychiatry.2017.3069

Tielbeek, J. J., Medland, S. E., Benyamin, B., Byrne, E. M., Heath, A. C., Madden, P. A., . . . Verweij, K. J. (2012). Unraveling the genetic etiology of adult antisocial behavior: A genome-wide association study. *PLoS One [Electronic Resource], 7*(10), e45086. https://dx.doi.org/10.1371/journal.pone.0045086

Tutton, R., & Levitt, M. (2010). Health and wealth, law and order: Banking DNA against disease and crime. In R. H. a. B. Prainsack (Ed.), *Genetic suspects: Global governance of forensic DNA profiling and databasing* (pp. 85–104). Cambridge, UK: Cambridge University Press.

Tuvblad, C., Narusyte, J., Comasco, E., Andershed, H., Andershed, A. K., Colins, O. F., . . . Nilsson, K. W. (2016). Physical and verbal aggressive behavior and COMT genotype: Sensitivity to the environment. *American Journal of Medical Genetics. Part B, Neuropsychiatric Genetics: The Official Publication of the International Society of Psychiatric Genetics, 171*(5), 708–718. doi:https://dx.doi.org/10.1002/ajmg.b.32430

Vayena, E., Salathe, M., Madoff, L. C., & Brownstein, J. S. (2015). Ethical challenges of big data in public health. *PLoS Computational Biology, 11*(2), e1003904. doi:10.1371/journal.pcbi.1003904

Wagner, S., Baskaya, O., Anicker, N. J., Dahmen, N., Lieb, K., & Tadic, A. (2010). The catechol o-methyltransferase (COMT) val(158)met polymorphism modulates the association of serious life events (SLE) and impulsive aggression in female patients with borderline personality disorder (BPD). *Acta Psychiatrica Scandinavica, 122*(2), 110–117. doi:https://dx.doi.org/10.1111/j.1600-0447.2009.01501.x

Waldby, C. (2009). Biobanking in Singapore: Post-developmental state, experimental population. *New Genetics and Society, 28*(3), 253–265. doi:10.1080/14636770903151943

Wallace, S. E., & Kent, A. (2011). Population biobanks and returning individual research results: Mission impossible or new directions? *Human Genetics, 130*(3), 393–401. doi:10.1007/s00439-011-1021-x

Wang, S., Jiang, X., Singh, S., Marmor, R., Bonomi, L., Fox, D., . . . Ohno-Machado, L. (2017). Genome privacy: Challenges, technical approaches to mitigate risk, and ethical considerations in the United States. *Annals of the New York Academy of Sciences, 1387*(1), 73–83. doi:10.1111/nyas.13259

Williams R., & Wienroth, M. (2014). Suspects, victims and others: Producing and sharing forensic genetic knowledge. *In R. Chadwick, M. Levitt, & D. Shickle (Eds.), The right to know and the right not to know: Genetic privacy and responsibility* (pp. 70–84). Cambridge, UK: Cambridge University Press.

Wolf, S. M., Crock, B. N., Van Ness, B., Lawrenz, F., Kahn, J. P., Beskow, L. M., . . . Wolf, W. A. (2012). Managing incidental findings and research results in genomic research involving biobanks and archived data sets. *Genetics in Medicine, 14*(4), 361–384. doi:10.1038/gim.2012.23

Zhang, W., Cao, C., Wang, M., Ji, L., & Cao, Y. (2016). Monoamine Oxidase A (MAOA) and Catechol-O-Methyltransferase (COMT) gene polymorphisms interact with maternal parenting in association with adolescent reactive aggression but not proactive aggression: Evidence of differential susceptibility. *Journal of Youth & Adolescence, 45*(4), 812–829. https://dx.doi.org/10.1007/s10964-016-0442-1

8 Big data

Generic roadmaps as global solutions for practice

Benoit Leclerc and Jesse Cale

Introduction

The ramifications of big data in practice are critical and countless. This phenomenon will persist through time, and corporate and non-corporate organisations, businesses and their executives, government agencies, scientists, universities, and the world in general are now starting to adapt, some reluctantly, others proactively. On the one hand, big data provides new possibilities in providing a virtual platform from which to build on, make new discoveries, and push the boundaries of collaboration within, between, and across organisations globally. People, individually and collectively, can now use data to further their learning and personal development, boost the development of businesses and collaborations locally or globally, and simply transform organisations. As Lee and Holt discussed in Chapter 6, those in charge of ensuring the security and protection of others, such as the police, now also benefit from more technological tools to conduct their work. On the other hand, big data also serves as a platform for those with malicious intentions. It provides individuals with criminal opportunities to also push boundaries in terms of capability and committing harms. Therefore, big data and analytics have the potential to generate innovation in the pursuit of good and the well-being of societies but also carry negative consequences, sometimes new forms of crimes, or more commonly, permitting certain crimes or inequities to proliferate. Regardless of the angle we take to approach big data and understand its impact on the world, big data is now an integral part of societies. In the end, it could be argued that the benefits and costs of big data neutralise each other to some extent – we are facing more complex problems, but we can also offer more sophisticated solutions.

The main aim of the current volume is to present a forward-thinking approach to the opportunities and challenges for the fields of criminology and criminal justice brought forth by the big data era. When commencing work on this volume, we drew on the business literature as we appreciated that big data, its challenges, and discussions on potential solutions to manage and benefit from it are currently given more prominent attention in this field than in academia in general, and criminology and criminal justice specifically. Throughout this exercise, most importantly, we also realised that the current volume has the power to not only guide the fields of criminology or criminal justice, but also those outside of academia, including both corporate and non-corporate organisations and government agencies. As a result, two roadmaps were developed to address culture and the research process and data analytics. From an organisational perspective, these roadmaps essentially fall under what is considered change management.

In an information era for which a defining characteristic has been described by many as a data deluge, it is without a doubt pertinent to adopt interdisciplinary and multidisciplinary approaches to problem solving. Furthermore, in the context of criminology and criminal justice, industry-academia partnerships are now more relevant than ever. One of the long-standing tensions between academia and industry in the context of criminology can be understood in terms of divergent goals in the two spheres. The goals of criminal justice are numerous, practical, and in some cases complementary, and in others, conflicting (e.g., punishment, rehabilitation, community safety, crime prevention, and so on). There is substantial pressure on criminal justice agencies and the professionals and practitioners in those agencies to get the 'right balance' on achieving these multiple and heterogeneous goals, and criminal justice agencies operate with increasingly limited budgets and human resources to do so. This context results in the additional pursuit for efficiency, and here, depending on political will and context, certain approaches may be favoured over others (e.g., crime control, rehabilitation, etc.).

A substantial part of academic criminology has been focused on understanding these contexts independent of engagement with industry to maintain a sense of objectivity or neutrality. For many, long-standing socio-structural inequities that arguably have favoured certain groups in society over others for generations are considered the key source of crime. Furthermore, in this context, criminal justice systems may be considered by many as a tool of colonial and patriarchal oppression that perpetuates inequity. There might be a certain degree of merit to such arguments depending on where one stands; criminal justice systems have not evolved substantially over the course of a couple centuries unlike many other social institutions. However, what is certain is that neglecting to engage with institutions such as the criminal justice system to work toward addressing these issues also means that the issues will persist well into the future. Furthermore, despite the substantial influence of politics in framing crime problems and criminal justice approaches, in the era of big data, we argue that it is becoming increasingly difficult, moreso than in the past, to overlook evidence on the factual basis for crime problems. Therefore, it is now more important than ever that criminology as an academic discipline strategically engages with the criminal justice system in order to improve efficiency, reduce inequity, and contribute to a just society. The key question remains as to how this can be done most effectively in the era of big data.

Drawing on the challenges related to big data articulated at the beginning of this volume, this concluding chapter is divided into two parts, each offering a generic roadmap to provide a systematic step-by-step process that can be adapted to any organisation and used as part of the solution for moving forward with big data. The first part provides a roadmap for creating or shaping the culture of an organisation toward facilitating a transition into big data. It is now becoming clear that big data and technological advances such as artificial intelligence do not represent the biggest challenges to organisations, but that culture does (Fountaine, McCarthy, & Saleh, 2019). The second part offers a roadmap to implement a systematic research process to collect relevant data, accumulate evidence-based knowledge, and translate the findings into practices that could improve organisations – the process that would typically follow transforming culture noting that many organisations may be gathering data without having necessarily a culture receptive to big data in the first place. With reason, the entry point and exit point of such a process have already been noted as critical in the business literature (Davenport, 2013). Once again, it is important to point out that the proposed roadmaps are generic and flexible in nature, and thus can be applied (and adapted if need be) to any organisation. While offering generic roadmaps applicable to any organisation, our discussion of these roadmaps will focus most closely on big data in criminology and criminal justice.

Roadmap for creating a culture receptive to big data

The six contributions from scholars across the fields of artificial intelligence, computing sciences, criminology, political science, and psychiatry all presented unique approaches and angles to investigate the utility of big data and data analytics moving forward in different criminology and criminal justice contexts. At the same time, despite the unique topics and contributions to the volume, certain key themes emerged organically across the chapters. Perhaps the most prominent theme that emerged across several of the chapters was that of culture. In the absence of an organisational culture that is receptive to engaging with data, the utility of introducing and engaging with big data and data analytics is virtually nil. These cultural challenges have existed in both academic criminology as well as criminal justice for some time and persist to this day. In terms of the former, this challenge starts in higher education with the lack of standardised research methods training across the discipline, from university to university, school to school, or program to program, which has resulted in a scenario where research methods 'expertise' among trained social scientists in criminology and criminal justice is characterised by much heterogeneity, ranging from virtually no actual research methods training to predominately qualitative research methods training to predominately quantitative research methods training, and very few practitioners with expertise across both areas.

This context contributes to unnecessary cultural divides in academic criminology and criminal justice programs and among those that situate quantitative and qualitative expertise as adversarial, rather than complementary; researchers in general often primarily identify as the general methodological approach they are inclined toward (i.e., 'quantitative researchers' or 'qualitative researchers'). In the era of big data, both lines of expertise will be optimal for two reasons: first, to understand how to work and boost our capabilities of working with big data effectively; and, second, to understand what big data can and cannot tell us in practice.

What's more, if these types of sub-disciplinary silos are evident within the field of criminology and criminal justice, long-standing disciplinary silos (e.g., across social sciences and related disciplines) present a challenge to effectively engaging with big data and analytics, for example, when it comes to resolving the complex ethical issues that emerge in the process, as Green pointed out in Chapter 7. In short, the need for multidisciplinary and interdisciplinary approaches has never been greater now that we have entered the big data era. It is necessary to foster cultures in criminology and criminal justice-related organisations to facilitate these approaches.

In criminal justice organisations specifically, cultural challenges to engaging with big data take somewhat of a different shape; the reluctance to engage with big data and data analytics stems for many from long standing traditions that have valued individual experience, expertise, and intuition over and above data. In the early days of criminal justice systems, around two centuries ago, this was likely sufficient; prior to and in the early years of the shift from agrarian to industrial societies that saw the introduction of formal criminal justice systems in Western industrialised nations, the populations being serviced were relatively small in number, culturally homogenous (i.e., relative to now), restricted to small geographical areas, and not particularly transient. Over the course of two hundred years, societies have developed dramatically; metropolitan centres are characterised by populations in the many millions, Western nations have become culturally heterogeneous, and crime has evolved to keep pace with commensurate opportunities these conditions have afforded. At the same time, overall, one may argue that criminal justice systems (i.e., law enforcement, courts, and corrections) do not look substantially different than they did a century or two ago. Perhaps the major exceptions to this are that across most Western nations, criminal justice systems are predominately characterised by increasing numbers of law enforcement personnel, substantial backlogs of court cases across judicial systems, and prisons that are routinely over capacity. The sheer size and scope of modern criminal justice systems means that it will take much more than an individuals' intuition, experience, and expertise to reform to a point where they become efficient and effective. It is necessary to move beyond the point of merely being critical and pointing out the challenges inherent in modern criminal justice systems, and to engage with these challenges to produce positive changes. Importantly, these challenges are complicated, and so too might be the solutions. One of the tools we increasingly have at our hands are big data and analytics, and as DeLisi pointed out in Chapter 2, the data are increasingly 'everywhere'. Furthermore, Skillicorn et al. (Chapter 5) showed that in the law enforcement context, not only can these data inform solutions to crime problems, but they can also be used to promote a standard of accountability in criminal justice. For this to happen effectively, however, requires cultures receptive to such aims, which could include methodologically trained subject area experts embedded in criminal justice systems to determine what big data can tell us in order to produce high quality evidence to effectively inform and improve criminal justice policy.

Culture is at the core of any major organisational changes or transformations. Of course, the need to shape a culture into one that is more receptive to data for instance may obviously vary within and across organisations and industries, but regardless, the challenge of culture is a central one. In order to raise awareness on the importance of creating a culture receptive to data, many principles have been highlighted in the business literature for this specific purpose (see Table 8.1). From the relevance of having culture 'catalysts' in an organisation to the need for securing the commitment of decision makers, these principles are all inter-connected and extremely valuable. This table, in part, led us to create roadmaps that can provide a systematic, applicable template to guide organisations step-by-step into making an effective transition into big data, or at least provide a framework with a sense of the steps that could possibly be followed during the transition.

Figure 8.1 presents a visual roadmap providing step-by-step guidance on how to navigate the process of creating a culture more receptive to big data. In the criminal justice context, as discussed earlier and alluded to throughout the volume, it is not uncommon to come across organisational cultures characterised by scepticism and reluctance toward the actual utility of data for decision-making. The first step is to understand the current culture of the organisation in relation to big data. This is important because understanding the basis for that mindset and why it exists will likely become more than obvious once an exploration of the history of the organisation, underlying values, subcultures, and leadership styles is conducted. This exploration can be achieved through internal sources, by meeting up with staff, and external channels, by examining reports or published data in public forums on the organisation. After this knowledge is accessible, it is possible to identify strengths and areas for improvement in an organisation and identify the best areas to target for improvement. The second step focuses on investigating the potential for a culture receptive to data. Determining the potential for a culture receptive to data can be achieved by meeting with key stakeholders on perceptions of big data and assessing the viability of the current environment for

Table 8.1 Principles related to establishing a culture receptive to data

Principle	Definition
Culture catalysts	People with ability to bridge data capabilities and organisation priorities
Data democratisation	Getting people excited about using data
Data culture is a decision culture	Improving decision making with evidence-based data
Data culture and risk	Awareness on the responsibility associated with introducing analytics into processes and systems
Marrying talent and culture	Integrating right talent for data culture
Commitment from executives	Need commitment from decision makers

Source: Diaz, Rowshankish, and Saleh (2018)

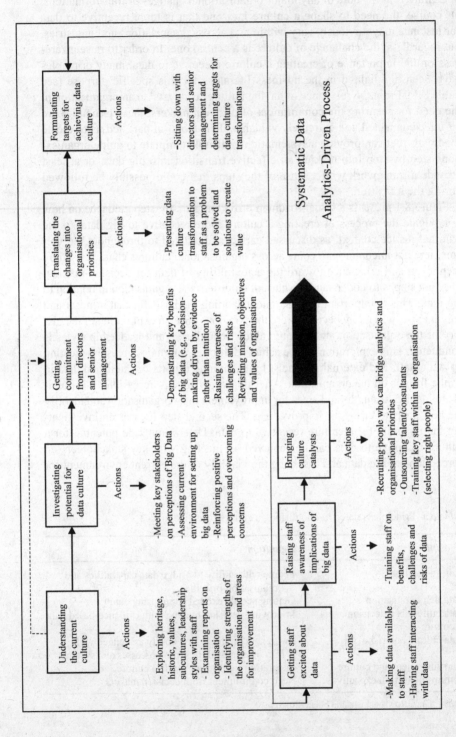

Figure 8.1 Roadmap for creating a culture receptive to data

Understanding the current culture

Actions

- Exploring heritage, historic, values, subcultures, leadership styles with staff
- Examining reports on organisation
- Identifying strengths of the organisation and areas for improvement

Investigating potential for data culture

Actions

- Meeting key stakeholders on perceptions of Big Data
- Assessing current environment for setting up big data
- Reinforcing positive perceptions and overcoming concerns

Getting commitment from directors and senior management

Actions

- Demonstrating key benefits of big data (e.g., decision-making driven by evidence rather than intuition)
- Raising awareness of challenges and risks
- Revisiting mission, objectives and values of organisation

Translating the changes into organisational priorities

Actions

- Presenting data culture transformation to staff as a problem to be solved and solutions to create value

Formulating targets for achieving data culture

Actions

- Sitting down with directors and senior management and determining targets for data culture transformations

Getting staff excited about data

Actions

- Making data available to staff
- Having staff interacting with data

Raising staff awareness of implications of big data

Actions

- Training staff on benefits, challenges and risks of data

Bringing culture catalysts

Actions

- Recruiting people who can bridge analytics and organisational priorities
- Outsourcing talent/consultants
- Training key staff within the organisation (selecting right people)

Systematic Data Analytics-Driven Process

big data. To be sure, we do not argue that a culture receptive to data can easily be transposed, or an organisational culture supporting it easily developed, but determining whether this is possible for cultural change is a crucial step. What we do argue is that where there is potential to develop (or improve) an organisational culture willing to engage with big data in a meaningful way, the benefits will outweigh the costs. To determine this, it is critical not only to assess buy-in from employees, managers, and so on, but also to be acutely aware of concerns that may exist among personnel and ensure that personnel have an

Related to the first two steps in the roadmap is ensuring that senior level management are committed to moving in a direction toward engaging more readily with data. At this step, presenting the key benefits to senior management and raising awareness on challenges and risks is imperative. Quite simply, if senior level management do not see benefit to their organisation, are not clear on the associated challenges and risks, and/or are unable to determine how engaging with big data and analytics can further the objectives of the organisation, trying to develop a culture receptive to data will likely be a futile exercise. It is likely that the mission, objectives, and values of the organisation will need consideration during this exercise. If there is organisational will to move toward a culture more receptive to data and evidence-based knowledge that has not existed previously, then this transformation needs to be presented as an organisational priority and challenge that needs to be solved – the following step. Staff and managers will need to understand the value of this transformation for the organisation to bring down barriers and concerns and ensure commitment. Once such a challenge is framed in this context, it is then necessary to develop solid achievable targets to move toward a more data-oriented organisational culture. This step will require sitting down with senior management and identifying reasonable targets for data culture transformation.

To many, data in general, and big data specifically, represent some sort of mythical information that can only be decoded by select few individuals (e.g., data analysts/scientists/statisticians). This likely ties into the scepticism discussed earlier, particularly in criminal justice agencies, that some may have toward the use of data for informed decision-making, and it makes sense. Having only a select few individuals who can access, collect/organise, analyse, and interpret data means that these few individuals hold the key to what the data say, and are additionally tasked with disseminating this information to everybody else. Furthermore, if these individuals do not communicate the data in accurate, strategic, and clear ways, or quite simply, if the rest of the people they are communicating to do not understand what the data say, these 'gate keepers' may find themselves outvoted or dismissed within an organisation, and decision-making may revert to popular vote based on consensus across individuals' experience, expertise, or intuition. Epistemologically, this process represents a collective regression from knowledge development through empiricism and observation to knowledge development based solely on intuition and/or tradition.

In order to avoid such situations, particularly if the goal is to build an organisational culture more receptive to big data and analytics, these processes need to be demystified. The next three steps in the roadmap are directed toward this aim and essentially represent the change management phase. The first involves getting individuals excited about data and its potential, and evidence-based knowledge more generally. This involves a process of data democratisation, namely, making data available to individuals within an organisation and also having them interact with it on a regular basis, rather than only having select few individuals act as gate keepers of big data and analytics. This step focuses on communicating the *what* of big data to its staff. Facilitated by this step, the next step will imply raising staff awareness on the implications of big data and analytics (i.e., challenges and benefits). Raising awareness can be achieved through introductory seminars and more specialised training on how to understand and work with data. We are not arguing here that all individuals in an organisation should be trained in data analytics, or conversely, that widespread training along these lines will mean that individuals with these specialist skills are no longer useful or required. Rather, we simply advocate for more wide-spread information and training to raise the collective 'bar' on individuals' comfort navigating, understanding, and interacting with data. This step focuses on communicating the why and how of big data to staff in the organisation.

One way to further facilitate these steps and boost change management is through the process of recruiting 'culture catalysts': strategically hired individuals with both substantive and technical skill sets in line with priorities around transforming into a data receptive organisational culture. Outsourcing expert consultants to increase staff capabilities temporarily is also a solution, as is selecting a few individuals in the organisation to act in this role. The reality is that individuals with 'culture catalyst' potential are rare. Therefore, a mix of these options appears a more feasible and realistic option. In criminal justice contexts, this also means individuals with training in criminology and criminal justice programs. However, as discussed earlier, criminology/criminal justice qualifications can take many different shapes and forms as post-secondary training in the field various dramatically across universities/schools/programs. Industries should be acutely aware of this, and in developing selection criteria for positions in the organisation, should be very clear on the key required attributes. While these will vary by organisation, perhaps the one constant we would argue for as a required attribute is comprehensive research methods training. Note, this does not solely reflect quantitative research training; obviously for some positions this will be required, but comprehensive methods training involves an in-depth understanding of the research process, research designs, and various methodologies. The point is not that an individual be an expert across these domains, but rather that they master the ability to learn and understand various approaches to research, which means they also have the aptitude to learn new ones. In turn, this builds and sets the stage for a research/data evidence-based literate organisation, and a stronger foundation for a culture that is adept at engaging with big data and analytics in novel ways that will benefit an organisation and improve the organisation's performance. This is the key focus of the following section.

Roadmap for implementing a systematic, data analytics-driven process

To the extent that evidence-based decision-making has been embraced by decision-makers in criminal justice, there is evidence to suggest the impacts have often been positive. For example, some evidence of the positive impact of evidence-based decision-making in criminal justice can be found in the adoption of proactive community-based law enforcement approaches, innovative court programs designed to divert individuals away from the criminal justice system, and innovative treatment and intervention programs for known offenders that have had demonstrable impacts, such as preventing offending or reducing the likelihood of reoffending. Key examples of success along these lines tell us that using high quality evidence and data can have demonstrable positive impacts on criminal justice policy. In the hands of properly trained experts, big data, and particularly novel analytics, also has the potential to 'investigate the hard questions', such as identifying whether and to what extent operational biases may exist in the provision of law enforcement services, as Skillicorn et al. demonstrated in Chapter 5. This in turn produces information that can be used to correct such problems if they exist. Of course, this is much easier said than done.

Possibly more often than anyone would like to admit, research is often conducted, whether in academic criminology or in criminal justice contexts, with key answers in mind prior to the research process, and a methodology that facilitates or reinforces the (re)discovery of these answers. Examples of this have been highlighted in practical contexts where research is commissioned to demonstrate the effectiveness of a treatment program or certain policy that is 'known' to work. This is antithetical to the scientific process of knowledge discovery, but nonetheless remains an easy and all-too-common trap to fall into. Therefore, in Figure 8.2, we revisit some basic concepts about the scientific process of research, with an eye toward providing guidance, particularly for those conducting research in industry, and how big data and analytics can fit into this process. A roadmap on implementing a systematic data analytics-driven process is proposed.

There are no shortages of challenges faced by different facets of criminal justice systems that are tasked with preventing offending; detecting and investigating crime; promoting community safety; ensuring fairness and due process of those suspected of committing crimes; incapacitating serious and violent individuals; ensuring proportional punishment of convicted offenders; addressing rehabilitation needs; and preventing re-offending, to name a few. Internally, criminal justice organisations face many similar issues to those of any business, arguably to a much larger extent, such as employee turnover, employee burnout, monitoring performance, regulation and compliance, competencies and recruiting the best talent, customer service, the pace of technological change, and, most pertinent for the current volume, how to deal with increasingly vast amounts of data and ensuring their integrity.

The first two steps in the roadmap in Figure 8.2 are incredibly important and intimately linked. The first of those steps is organisational challenge. It involves

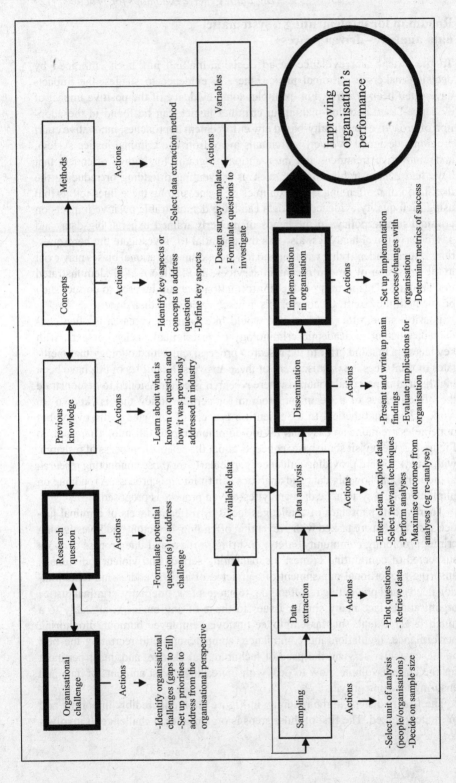

Figure 8.2 Roadmap for implementing a systematic data analytics–driven process

identifying a specific challenge(s) that an organisation seeks to investigate and overcome through a systematic data analytics-driven process that is in line with broader organisational priorities, whether they are internal or external, as well as its mission and values. This step may most likely require asking many questions to the organisation in order to ensure that the challenge(s) are accurately identified, and the priorities correctly set up. In order to set up the right priorities, some initial exploration may be required if data already exist. The next step in the process is to formulate researchable (or 'addressable') questions to address the challenge and the priorities that were identified in step one, and next, determine whether and to what extent data exist to answer the questions. This is one of the most important steps in the process, particularly considering the context of big data, and one with which most organisations would struggle. Here, consistent with identifying the challenge and setting up the priorities, we expect that organisations will need to sit down and tailor the questions according to the mission and objectives of their respective organisation. In this sense, the questions at first do not need to be 'perfect' at all. Questions are often refined during such a process where data that were initially thought to be irrelevant may become relevant. While it is important to not use data that do not fit the questions, it is also essential to remember that it may be worth exploring the data in hand if it exists. This process may actually feedback into formulating 'researchable' questions to examine for the organisation, and in the end, speed up the process leading to a positive outcome for an organisation.

However, just because an organisation collects vast amounts of data, this does not necessarily mean that these data are automatically well suited to answer certain research questions or even be used all together. It is important to avoid the tendency to revise important research questions to fit the data available to analyse them; a common adage in first year research methods courses in social sciences is: 'garbage in = garbage out', and this must be applied here. The quality and appropriateness of data is paramount to gaining valid answers to research questions. If the data are not suited to a particular question that carries substantial organisational importance, even if there is a lot of it, it is probably in the best interest to collect new or complementary data. One way to assess whether and to what extent the data may be suited to answering a research question is by finding out what is already known about the question, how it has been researched in the past, and what kinds of data were utilised in previous contexts. For example, corrective services are quite often interested in what programs for prisoners are effective in reducing reoffending outcomes post-release. Of course, there is robust international literature on evaluations of different programs delivered by corrective services from around the world that employ many different research designs and data sources. It is important to note that rarely will the data, whether already available or to be gathered, be 'readily applicable'. In most contexts, formulating the right questions will most likely imply finding the right equilibrium between the context and objectives of the organisation and 'good enough' data.

The next step involves identifying concepts that are measurable to answer the research question. For example, in the context of evaluating the effectiveness of a prison program, what is meant by post-release outcome? Probably the most common post-release outcome that is employed by studies is that of reoffending, whether measured by new charges, convictions, and/or returns to custody, all of which are routinely collected administrative data and obtained through either law enforcement or corrective services. However, numerous other post release outcomes are not routinely collected, especially if an individual does not return to the criminal justice system. For example, these can include employment, entering a stable relationship, joining a community organisation, volunteering, and so on. The point is that it is important to clearly identify key concepts in research that are measurable and understand what aspects of the research question they do and do not inform.

Once the research question(s) is finalised and key concepts are operationalised, the question of data extraction enters the picture. Are high quality and appropriate data already available to adequately investigate the research question posed, and elucidate the necessary concepts that have been operationalised in a specific fashion? If the answer is yes, then these data need to be extracted from larger databases held within an organisation. A common mistake made when vast amounts of data are available in this context is the tendency to believe that they all need be analysed in their entirety to produce a robust analysis. Again, if well-grounded research questions have been developed, and the variables adequately operationalised, then data extraction should involve those key variables pertinent to answering the research questions, which better fits the reality of generating outcomes rapidly enough for organisations to make the best of the data in the short-term. If these key variables are unavailable or there are other issues (e.g., large amounts of missing data), then it is necessary to develop another instrument or tool to collect/acquire the appropriate data or simply design and include the variables needed into the current process.

Whether the data are readily available or a new data collection procedure (e.g., an online survey) is developed, a clearly defined sampling frame may be necessary to extract the most optimal sample to analyse the research question. In an administrative data set, for example, this might include all of the relevant cases, whatever the units of analysis may be, over a certain time period, in a certain jurisdiction, and so on. In the context of big data, sampling increasingly involves ALL cases, but even so, ALL cases are typically restricted to certain time periods for which data exist or specific geographic areas, etc. In effect, this decision once again goes back to the research question and what the best data available are to answer it. Therefore, it is also necessary that there is clarity around the units of analysis. Is the research question concerned with people? Organisations? Incidents? Once the unit of analysis is selected and the sample is clearly defined, then data extraction can take place; data can be retrieved within the specified parameters described earlier, or, in the case that a new tool such as a survey is developed to collect data, pilot testing of the instrument can take place.

Much time and effort in research projects is often spent focusing on data analytic decisions and deciding on analytic/statistical techniques to analyse data, often from the outset of projects. Importantly, as Figure 8.2 shows, this is in fact one small element of the broader roadmap. We also argue that while it is clearly important data analysis is done properly, this element of the roadmap is the least crucial because if data analyses are incorrect, they can be redone and corrected much easier than if crucial errors in any of the previous steps are evident. In effect, if there are critical errors or limitations in data collection, operationalising variables, or sampling, there is much higher risk to the overall project fidelity than if a correctable data analysis error is made. Note that in the upper steps of the roadmap there are more bidirectional arrows, indicating that these steps are more of an iterative process involving a cycle of activities in order to fine tune, but the roadmap becomes more streamlined from this point on, particularly once data have been collected. Furthermore, there are a multitude of different ways to analyse data, some more robust than others, and decisions around what data analysis techniques to use have as much to do with research questions as they do with the levels of measurement of variables, distributions of variables, and missing data. Therefore, while data analysis decisions are crucial, they will also be the least relevant if the prior steps of the roadmap are compromised; again, 'garbage in = garbage out'.

The end of the roadmap for generating empirical evidence from big data in order to improve an organisation's performance involves the dissemination of the findings and what these mean for the organisation – the most critical step along with the first and second steps of the process (the entry and exit points highlighted by Davenport, 2013). This is the stage where evidence-informed (i.e., based on research) implementation processes and changes can be actioned. Again, these may be internal (e.g., new organisational policy) or external (e.g., evidence to inform programs offered to clients by the organisation) to an organisation, but without the communication of the research results any actionable change will be unlikely to occur. What's more, if research results are not communicated in a fashion that is appropriate to the specific target audience, the research again runs the risk of failing to see any resultant actionable change or impact. As an example, research presented at academic conferences, typically, will look very different from research presented to policy makers, or to internal members of an organisation, or to the public. In the academic context, when it comes to the dissemination of research, much time and effort is spent on communicating important methodological details to open the research to scrutiny and feedback surrounding how robust the findings are and the validity of the conclusions put forth. While this is clearly important to any research, in the policy context, of primary relevance are the findings and implications of the research, along with the presumption that the methodology is robust and the findings valid. The reason for and implications of research are typically also very important to internal members of an organisation for whom the research may directly affect. Finally, communicating results of research to the public is often typically scaled down with a focus on key findings and broader implications. Regardless of the audience, the point is that the dissemination of research needs to be tailored to the appropriate audiences; otherwise its impact will likely be diminished.

In the last step, setting up an implementation process for change based on the findings arising from analytics may in fact depend as much on the effective dissemination and communication of the results as it does on the research itself. As part of the implementation of any transformation, a plan to evaluate the changes will need to be developed, as well as the metrics for success, which may involve setting up and monitoring KPIs. In short, evidence that is quantifiable will need to be collected to determine the extent of the success of the implementation. For instance, data analytics could be used to gather insights on the skills and interests of staff and link those to high performance as a priority for the organisation based on its mission, values, and objectives. Then several positions could be allocated to staff accordingly into the roles that will maximise individual and professional growth and success and, as a result, generate better outcomes for the organisation (Davenport, Harris, & Shapiro, 2010).

Conclusion

Big data entails a major disruption in the ways we think about and do things, which certainly applies to most organisations, including those operating in the criminology and criminal justice fields. It is fascinating to observe that despite the unique topics and contributions to this volume, the most prominent theme that emerged across several of the chapters was that of culture. As pointed out before, the absence of an organisational culture, whether in academic criminology or criminal justice, that is receptive to engaging with big data, or simply data period, the utility of introducing and engaging with big data and data analytics may prove to be irrelevant, or perhaps at worst, a costly exercise for organisations.

Big data is currently disrupting processes in most organisations: how different organisations collaborate with one another, how organisations develop products or services, how organisations can quickly scale up their business, how organisations can identify, recruit, and evaluate talent, how organisations can compete with one another, how organisations can make better decisions based on empirical evidence rather than intuition, and how organisations can quickly implement any transformation plan, to name a few. All of these processes are important to tap into, but two underlying processes are critical to establish a foundation that will permit organisations to flourish and thrive in the era of big data – creating a culture more receptive to big data and implementing a systematic, data analytics-driven process within the organisation.

Creating roadmaps on culture and the data analytics process emerged as critical after reading and making sense of the business literature on big data and compiling the work of the contributors of the current volume. There is one clear objective underlying these roadmaps: change management – guiding, and working with, organisations (criminal justice-related or not) to facilitate transitions into and management of big data. While big data may involve challenges which we are not currently aware of, creating a culture more receptive to big data is no doubt a priority and a critical starting point for any organisation. There is no assumption here that all the challenges and benefits of big data have been covered in this volume. Another volume could probably be written on big data, especially given how rapidly it is changing the ways we think about and do things on a day-to-day basis. In this sense, this volume also represents an invitation to all to engage with big data and analytics for generating positive outcomes.

References

Davenport, T. H. (2013, July–August). Keep up with your quants. *Harvard Business Review*, 120–123.

Davenport, T. H., Harris, J., & Shapiro, J. (2010, October). Competing on talent analytics. *Harvard Business Review*, 52–58.

Diaz, A., Rowshankish, K., & Saleh, T. (2018, September). Why data culture matters? *McKinsey Quarterly*, 1–17.

Fountaine, T., McCarthy, B., & Saleh, T. (2019, July–August). Building the AI-powered organization. *Harvard Business Review*, 63–73.

Index

Note: Page numbers in **bold** indicate tables; page numbers in *italics* indicate figures.

Printed in the United States
By Bookmasters